Language is like a vast spider's web. In this volume Jean Aitchison explores different facets of this web. She begins with the cobweb of false worries which surrounds language. She then discusses how language evolved in the human species, how children acquire it, and how educated English speakers remember 50,000 or more words. Finally, she argues that people are right to be concerned about language, though not in the ways traditionally assumed.

This is the text of the 1996 BBC Reith lectures, slightly revised for publication, with illustrations and full references, and an Afterword which looks at the reception of the lectures.

The language web

Published by the Press Syndicate of the University of Cambridge
The Pitt Building, Trumpington Street, Cambridge CB2 1RP
40 West 20th Street, New York, NY 10011–4211, USA
10 Stamford Road, Oakleigh, Melbourne 3166, Australia

First published 1997

Printed in the United Kingdom at the University Press, Cambridge

Illustrations: Priscilla Barrett
Graphics: Malcolm Forbes

A catalogue record for this book is available from the British Library

Library of Congress cataloguing in publication data applied for

ISBN 0 521 573858 hardback
ISBN 0 521 574757 paperback

Contents

Preface

All normal human beings talk. Many find it hard to imagine living without language, so much so that they sometimes fantasize about a world in which animals can speak, as when a character in a children's storybook encountered a chattering toad:

> 'Can you really talk?' she whispered. The toad raised his drooping head a little. 'I have been talking since I was a mere tadpole,' he said huffily.

Language, then, is taken for granted. But its nearness and naturalness cause two problems. First, people do not usually spend time observing it. The situation is somewhat like that in a Sherlock Holmes story, in which the fictional detective questioned a visitor about a flight of stairs:

> 'You have frequently seen the steps which lead up from the hall to this room... how many are there?'
> 'How many! I don't know.'
> 'Quite so!' said Sherlock. 'You have not observed. And yet you have seen. That is just my point. Now, I know that there are seventeen steps, because I have both seen and observed.'

Similarly, language speakers see, but they do not observe. More accurately, they hear, but they do not perceive. Language is all

around them, but most are unable to answer even straightforward questions, such as 'When do children become competent
speakers?' 'How do language changes happen?', and so on.

The second problem overlaps with the first. Because everyone talks, many confidently assume that they can therefore pronounce authoritatively on their language. This is somewhat
puzzling. After all, humans breathe, but they do not therefore
assume that they know about breathing: they go to a doctor, or
read a biology book. Yet because they talk, many *do* feel able to
comment on linguistic matters, and often have surprising confidence in the rightness of their views. As a result, various
entrenched beliefs circulate. Some of them are clear cut and
wrong, such as the folk-myth that Eskimos have hundreds of
words for snow. Others are vague and ill-defined, such as the
widespread assumption that something called 'proper English'
exists, a variety of language which educated speakers ought to
know. When quizzed, people are typically unclear what this
'proper English' consists of, whether it is spoken, or written,
or who actually makes use of it. Anyone pressed on the point
often proposes prohibitions, usually quite trivial ones, such as:
'If you speak proper English, you shouldn't split infinitives',
even though split infinitives are widely used, as in *to humbly
apologize, to sexually assault, to boldly confront*, nor do they
cause any inclarity. In fact, an unsplit infinitive may be less
clear than a split one, as in 'He decided to go boldly to confront
his tormentor', where it is unclear whether *boldly* is attached
to *go* or *confront* or perhaps both. In short, various strictures are
widespread, and are based on a strange mix: memories of old

schoolbooks, uneasiness about language change, alongside a commonsense realization that 'anything goes' is too broad – though what might go where and when is not usually specified.

A strong interest in language by so many people is enormously pleasing. But the general lack of knowledge is worrying, though perhaps understandable. Linguistics, the study of language, was a late starter in our universities. The first university undergraduate course in linguistics in Great Britain began only in the late 1960s, though somewhat earlier in the United States. Linguistic findings which are widely known within the field have only relatively recently begun to filter through to schools, and to the rest of the population.

Meanwhile 'Why-o-why, isn't it a disgrace?' letters about language are still commonplace in newspapers, even though the wording of many of these letters suggests that their writers were educated a long time ago, and have had minimal opportunities to learn about modern views on language. This perpetuation of old ideas is combined with a no doubt healthy suspicion that academics should not be believed without question.

Yet knowledge about language truly has taken several bunny-hops forward in this century. And I am privileged to have had the opportunity to talk about some of these advances to a wide audience of radio listeners via the 1996 BBC Reith lectures. These lectures were inaugurated in 1948 in honour of Lord Reith, director general of the BBC from 1927 to 1938. The topics change. The first set was given by Bertrand Russell, and those in 1995 by the architect Sir Richard Rogers. In 1996, it was the turn of language.

Preface

My lecture plan was straightforward. 'The language web' was the title: webs can both enable and ensnare, they have a pre-ordained overall pattern, and the various strands form an interlinked whole. The cobweb of false worries which surrounds language was the topic of my first lecture. In my next three lectures, I discussed how language evolved in the human species, how children acquire it, and how educated English speakers remember 50,000 or more words. Finally, I stressed that people are right to be concerned about language, though not in the ways traditionally assumed.

With my first lecture, I unwittingly banged the linguistic funny bone of Radio 4 regulars, and also some journalists. The response amazed me. My delight at those who enjoyed the lectures was mixed with astonishment at those who ranted at me – all quite puzzling to someone who works at Oxford, where lectures mostly pass unnoticed unless they are directly usable in examinations. But the furore gradually died down, and as the lectures proceeded, they evoked less agitation, and more support.

Yet the volume of press coverage and letters I received surprised me. When I finally counted the comments in the press (getting on for one hundred), and the letters (getting on for two hundred), I discovered that a large number of correspondents simply wanted more information about language: could I tell them my sources for comments on the use of *he* for 'he or she', for example, or where could they find out more about children acquiring a language that was not English? I answered as many queries as I could in personal letters to those who asked. But many more busy people might exist who heard some of the lectures, and who had queries, but who did not have the time to write. I have therefore tried to provide additional information within this book.

This book of the lectures is the broadcast text with some extra paragraphs and occasional illustrations in place of the original sound effects. It also includes a survey of responses from journalists and correspondents. In addition, full notes give sources of work referred to in the text, as well as suggestions for further reading. Hopefully, readers will see the book of the lectures as a stepping-stone towards a broader overall knowledge of language.

My thanks go to the numerous people who helped me in the preparation of both the lectures and this book, perhaps above all to the BBC producer Tessa Watt, many of whose valuable suggestions were incorporated into the final version; to my research assistant Diana Lewis who helped check out references and prepare the final manuscript; and to my partner John Ayto who patiently cooked and comforted as I wrote and re-wrote the lectures. Numerous other people contributed in various ways, at the BBC, in Oxford, and from around the world, by helping to provide sound effects, answering my questions, responding to my ideas, and so on. And a huge amount of thanks go also to Cambridge University Press, particularly Judith Ayling and Lin Vasey, who by hard work and helpfulness have managed to produce this book in a fraction of the normal time.

Jean Aitchison
Oxford 1996

Acknowledgements

For kind permission to quote from copyright material the author is grateful to the following: Geoffrey Wagner, *The Wisdom of Words* (George Allen & Unwin, an imprint of HarperCollins Publishers Limited); Martin Amis, *London Fields* (Peters Fraser & Dunlop Group Ltd); 'Listen Mr Oxford Don' in *Mangoes and Bullets*, © John Agard (Serpent's Tail, London); Penelope Lively, *Moon Tiger* (Penguin UK); and Vladimir Nabokov, *Pale Fire* (Weidenfeld & Nicolson Ltd).

❶ A web of worries

Anxiety about language

Personally I wish someone had told me . . . in my youth that . . . language is primarily speech and only secondarily writing. I wish someone had also told me that most grammar texts are so many etiquette books, and accepted usage a dialect of middle-class residents of a capital city . . .

The truth is that 'rules' never existed, they have little to do with language. They were superimposed on organic word-wisdom by a set of largely clerical-minded inkhorns standing around with a lot of egg on their faces.

Geoffrey Wagner The wisdom of words (1968)

Is our language sick? You might think so, judging from complaints: 'The standard of speech and pronunciation in England has declined so much . . . that one is almost ashamed to let foreigners hear it', moaned a writer in a daily newspaper. 'The language the world is crying out to learn is diseased in its own country', ranted another. 'We are plagued with idiots on radio and television who speak English like

the dregs of humanity, to the detriment of our children',
lamented yet another.

But why? At a time when English is a major world language,
is it really in need of hospital treatment? A wide web of worries,
a cobweb of old ideas, ensnares people as they think about language – any language – and this must be swept away.

But clearing the cobwebs is only the first stage. *The language web* is the overall title of this book. Webs, especially
cobwebs, may entangle. Yet webs themselves are not a tangle.
They have a preordained overall pattern, though every one is
different in its details. Nature forces humans to weave the language web in a particular way, whatever language they speak.
We are free only within a preset framework. The outline plan
of language is fixed, part of our genetic inheritance. So liberty
within limits will be a major theme. Another will be the interlinked nature of the various strands. I shall look at some key
linguistic topics which illustrate these themes: how language
changes, how it began, how children learn it, and how we
remember words.

But first, the cobweb of worries must be removed. This
envelops all of language, though especially language change.
Yet humpback whales alter their songs every year, and nobody
has complained.

Naturally, language changes all the time. This is a fact of life.
In the fourteenth century, Geoffrey Chaucer noted that *in forme
of speche is chaunge* 'language changes' (see figure 1.1), and the
same is true today. But change is one thing. Decay is another. Is
our language really changing for the worse, as some people argue?

Ye knowe ek, that in forme of speche is chaunge
'You know too, that in form of speech there's change

Withinne a thousand yer, and wordes tho
Within a thousand years, and words which in their day

That hadden prys now wonder nyce and straunge
Once had strong values, now seem weak and strange.

Us thenketh hem, and yet they spake hem so,
Yet people truly talked in that old way:

And spedde as wel in love as men now do.
In love, they fared as well as folk today.'

Geoffrey Chaucer, Troylus and Criseyde

1.1 In forme of speche is chaunge

Of course not. Over a hundred years ago, linguists – those who work on linguistics, the study of language – realized that different styles of language suit different occasions, but that no part of language is ever deformed or bad. People who dispute this are like cranks who argue that the world is flat. Yet flat-earth views about language are still widespread. As the Swiss linguist Ferdinand de Saussure said over seventy-five years ago: 'No other subject has spawned more absurd ideas, more prejudices, more illusions or more myths.' Things have not changed very much since then.

On inspection, the web of worries surrounding change turns out to be largely traditional, somewhat like the worries each new generation of parents has about its offspring. Laments about language go back for centuries.

A fourteenth-century monk complained that the English practise *strange wlaffyng, chytering, harryng, and garryng gris-bittyng* 'strange stammering, chattering, snarling and grating tooth-gnashing'. And the complaints continued. 'Tongues, like governments, have a natural tendency to degeneration', wrote the lexicographer Samuel Johnson, in the preface to his famous *Dictionary of the English language* published in 1755.

Eighteenth-century worries are perhaps understandable. Around 1700, the seemingly fixed grammar of Latin aroused great admiration, at a time when English itself was in a fairly fluid state. Many people hoped to lay down similar firm precepts for English, and assumed that somebody, somewhere, knew what 'correct English' was. Jonathan Swift wrote a famous letter to the Lord Treasurer in 1712 urging the formation of an academy to regulate language usage. He complained that 'many gross improprieties' could be found in the language of 'even the best authors'. But 'correct English' was as hard to define then as it is now. In practice upper- and middle-class speech was often praised as 'good', artificially supplemented by precepts from logic and imitations of various Latin usages. As long ago as 1789, the dictionary writer Noah Webster commented: 'Had the English never been acquainted with Greek and Latin they would never have thought of one half the distinctions and rules which make up our English grammar.' These invented rules often get confused with genuine language rules.

All languages have their own 'rules' in the sense of recurring, subconscious patterns. In English, we usually place the verb inside the sentence, and say: 'The spider caught the fly.' In Welsh, the verb comes first: 'Caught the spider the fly' *Daliodd y pryf copyn y gleren*, and in Turkish it comes last, 'The spider the fly caught', or 'A bottle of good wine I want' *Bir şişe iyi şarap istiyorum*. Without these real rules, communication would break down: 'Henry ate an octopus' does not mean the same as 'An octopus ate Henry.'

But real rules or patterns need to be distinguished from artificially imposed ones. For example, an old and illogical belief that logic should govern language has led in English to a ban on the double negative, as in 'I don't know nothing', which is now standardly: 'I don't know anything.' This is odd, because in most languages of the world, the more negatives, the stronger the negation. This was true in thirteenth-century English.

Chaucer, in the *Canterbury Tales*, said of the courteous knight, roughly: 'He never said no bad thing to nobody.' In Chaucer's words:

> He *nevere* yet *no* vileyne *ne* sayde
> In all his lyf unto *no* maner wight.
> He was a verray, parfit gentil knyght.

The prohibition on double negatives may have begun with Robert Lowth, an eighteenth-century Bishop of London, who wrote a *A short introduction to English grammar*. In it he stated that 'two Negatives in English destroy one another, or are equivalent to an affirmative'. Perhaps his high status as a bishop led people to believe that his strictures on language were divinely inspired. The ban stuck. In the late nineteenth century, for example, John Earle, an educator, commented: 'The student . . . is instructed how contrary to reason is a Double Negative.' Yet it never entirely disappeared. It is still found in some varieties of English, as in the old music hall song: 'We don't know no one wot don't want no nine inch nails.'

Another artificially imposed rule involves *different to*. 'I am irritated by the frequent use of the words *different to* on radio and other programmes', huffed a letter to a daily paper. 'In my schooldays of fifty years ago we were taught that things were *alike to* and *different from*. Were our teachers so terribly ignorant?' Yet *different to* is found even in the seventeenth century. 'How much different art thou to this curs'd spirit here', said the dramatist Thomas Dekker, in 1603. The *Oxford English Dictionary* lists several other examples of *different to,* and a preference for *different from* is labelled a 'superstition' by Fowler in 1926 in his widely admired book *Modern English usage.* Some of these old invented prohibitions remind one of Alice in Wonderland, who complained to the king: 'That's not a regular rule, you invented it just now.'

Moving on to the nineteenth century, proper behaviour was a major concern to a lot of people. Etiquette books were popular, and precepts about language were issued alongside advice about table manners. Consider some of the instructions in *Don't. A manual of mistakes and improprieties more or less prevalent in conduct and speech*, which was published around 1880:

> Don't drink too much wine. Don't drink from your saucer . . .
> Don't wear diamonds in the morning. Don't neglect the small
> hairs that project from the nostrils and grow about the apertures
> of the ears . . . Don't say gents for gentlemen, nor pants for pan-
> taloons. These are inexcusable vulgarisms. Don't say transpire
> when you mean occur. Don't say 'loads of time' or 'oceans of time'
> . . . Say 'ample time' or 'time enough'. Don't use a plural pronoun
> when a singular is called for . . . 'Everybody put on their hats' . . .
> illustrates a prevalent error . . . Don't say 'It is him,' say 'It is he . . .'

And so on, and so on. Yet some of these injunctions are at odds with history. The 'prevalent error' of mixing singular and plural pronouns is a usage of long standing: 'If a person is born of a gloomy temper . . . they cannot help it', said the Earl of Chesterfield in the eighteenth century (see figure 1.2).

Some of these artificial rules have been passed down from generation to generation. Their main effect is to make people insecure, to worry that they might not be using the right phrase,

Anyone ... they

Eighteenth century

If a person is born of a ... gloomy temper ... THEY cannot help it. *Earl of Chesterfield*

Nineteenth century

A person can't help THEIR birth. *William Thackeray*

But how can you talk with a person if THEY always say the same thing? *Lewis Carroll*

Early twentieth century

I know when I like a person directly I see THEM. *Virginia Woolf*

Nobody would ever marry if THEY thought it over. *George Bernard Shaw*

Late twentieth century

If somebody earns $40,000 a year we would expect THEM to pay for their course. *A University Vice-Chancellor*

We are looking for a young man or woman in THEIR mid-twenties ... *Job advertisement*

If anyone calls, tell THEM I'm at a meeting ... *Often heard instruction*

AND I THOUGHT ALL THIS WAS MODERN DECADENCE!

1.2 A long-standing usage

just as they might get anxious that they are not using the right type of spoon for soup. Again and again, etiquette, morals and speech are confused. *Groombridge's Annual Reader*, a manual of recitation 'for the use of schools' said in 1867: 'Speech is a gift of God . . . and the habit of speaking correct English . . . next to good morals, is one of the best things in the world.'

We might laugh at this quaint confusion of morals and speech, except that it is still found nowadays. In 1985, 'bad English', whatever that might be, was even linked to crime by Norman Tebbit, then a key British government figure. He said:

> If you allow standards to slip to the stage where good English is no better than bad English, where people turn up filthy . . . at school . . . all those things tend to cause people to have no standards at all, and once you lose standards then there's no imperative to stay out of crime.

This tangled web of worries around language shows that many people, including some of those in positions of power, are back in the dark ages over understanding how it works.

But it would be oversimple to lump all language worries together, and just dismiss them. The different strands of worry need to be teased out. Above all, three overlapping accusations recur, which can be called the 'damp spoon' syndrome, the 'crumbling castle' view, and the 'infectious disease' assumption.

The 'damp spoon' image comes from a British newspaper writer who had a 'queasy distaste' for the 'vulgarity' of some current usages, 'precisely the kind of distaste I feel at seeing a damp spoon dipped in the sugar bowl or butter spread with the bread-knife'. She implies that sloppiness and laziness cause much of language change.

The notion that change is due to laziness has been around for a long time. In the last century, the linguist Max Müller argued that 'the principal cause of phonetic degeneracy in language is when people shrink from articulating each consonant and vowel; when they attempt to economize their breath and their muscular energy . . . If the provincial of Gaul came to say *père* instead of *pater*, it was simply because he shrank from the trouble of lifting his tongue, and pushing it against his teeth.' But omission of *t* within a word is unlikely to be due to laziness. In British English, the pronunciation of *bu'er* with a glottal stop in place of older *butter* is often heard. But *Be'y 'ad a bi' of bi'er bu'er* for older 'Betty had a bit of bitter butter' requires considerable muscular tension, and cannot be regarded as a lazy development.

The only truly lazy speech is drunken speech, where alcohol affects coordination, and English is not getting like drunken speech. Some years ago, researchers at the University of Texas checked this out. They plied student volunteers with slugs of neat whiskey every twenty minutes for six hours, and before each new drink, they asked the students to read a word list and chat. They found that the bumbles and mumbles of drunkards were fairly unlike the alterations in normal change. Drunken people keep vowels much the same, but lengthen consonants, which get dragged out. They are also likely to pronounce *s* and *ch* as *sh*, so *yes* comes out as *yesh*, and *church* as *shersh*. These effects are due to a temporary lack of muscular coordination, and are not happening in English as a whole.

Tense-endings are quite often omitted in spoken speech. A sentence written as *Pamela jumped back* is likely to be pronounced as *Pamela jump back*, or *Peter climbed carefully down* as *Peter climb carefully down*. This is sometimes claimed to be 'laziness'. But these omissions usually take place when three consonants come together. The omission of the middle consonant enables speech to be speeded up, and is unlikely to destroy the meaning. So there's a trade-off between smooth, fast speech, and slow, careful, jerky speech. Faster speech involves more words per minute, and cannot be classed as 'laziness'.

Of course, fast speech forms occur mostly in casual conversation. But informal speech is not intrinsically 'worse' than formal speech, it is just different. Humans naturally adapt their speech to suit the situation: they slow it down for babies and strangers, and they speed it up for friends. Eventually, some of these fast speech changes will creep into all types of speech. Only actors pronounce *handbag* as it's written, most famously in Oscar Wilde's play *The importance of being earnest*, when Lady Bracknell, acted by Edith Evans, expressed shock and horror that the young man to whom she was talking had as a baby been found abandoned in a handbag. 'A handbag!!!' she exclaims in horror, lingering over each sound. Almost everybody else says *hambag*. Once a change of this type has occurred, hearers often judge the older, outmoded form to be pedantic and less 'streamlined'.

The language web

The 'crumbling castle' view is a second common accusation. This treats the English language as a beautiful old building with gargoyles and pinnacles which need to be preserved intact, as implied in statements by the writer John Simon. Language, he argues, should be treated like 'parks, national forests, monuments, and public utilities . . . available for properly respectful use but not for defacement or destruction'. This view crumbles when examined carefully. It implies that the castle of English was gradually and lovingly assembled until it reached a point of maximum splendour at some unspecified time in the past. Yet no year can be found when language achieved some peak of perfection, like a vintage wine. Nor have those who claim that English is declining ever suggested what this date might have been.

Furthermore, the 'beautiful building' notion presupposes that rigid systems, once assembled, are better than changing ones. This is untrue. In the animal world, flexibility is a great advantage, and animals which adhere to fixed systems often lose out. Consider the blue-footed booby, a sea-bird which lives on the Galapagos Islands. This gannet behaves according to a rule of thumb: 'In the nest feed it; out of the nest ignore it.' So if a young booby falls out of its nest, it inevitably dies, even when the nest is at ground level. A less rigid system might allow the parent boobies to assess whether or not the squawking displaced youngster was one of their own, and if so, push it back into the nest. But the booby's rigid system does not allow for this.

The ever-shifting nature of language keeps it flexible, so it

can cope with changing social circumstances, as with the rush
of new words relating to cars in the twentieth century, such as
the recent *autochondria* from 'automobile' and 'hypochondria'
– someone with excessive concern for the health of their car.

'Crumbling castle' supporters might argue that such addi-
tions are trivial and allowable, as long as older forms are preserved alongside. But in the long run, this is impossible, as
shown by the increasing loss of old past tense forms, which
provide a clear example of how earlier forms get whittled away.
First, the old irregular forms gradually get forgotten, especially
when the verbs are rarely used ones. In this century, *gelded* and
girded have mostly replaced *gelt* and *girt* as the past tense forms
of *geld* and *gird,* and many people don't even realize a change
has occurred. Replacement can happen even with better known
verbs. The American clothes designer Donna Karan, discussing
the letters she received, said: 'Anything that *beared* my name,
I'd open': in her speech, *beared* has apparently replaced older
bore as the past tense of *bear.* Second, new uses of old forms
tend to acquire regular endings, as in *shoot up* of drugs:
'Someone passed me this syringe . . . and I shooted up', said a
drug-taker quoted in *The Guardian* newspaper. Third, any new
forms receive regular inflections, as in the term *bland out*
'become conformist': 'Those that didn't burn out, *blanded out*',
according to a writer in the *New Musical Express.* So more and
more old forms are wiped away as new, regular forms flood in.
But this is not disintegration. Sweeping up old bits and pieces is
good housekeeping, or rather good language-keeping. Gradual
neatening up of patterns is inevitable and essential. In this way,

the mind avoids becoming overloaded with unpredictable oddments.

Neatening up also happens with nouns. *Houses* were once *housen* and *shoes* were *shooen*, parallel to *oxen*. Imported words get tidied up too. The Italian word *graffito* 'scratch' has been in use in English for well over a century, usually in the plural *graffiti*, meaning 'scratches or scribbles on walls'. Recently, this plural has begun to be treated as if it were the singular: *Graffiti is disgusting* proclaimed an official notice on a London bus. Not everyone likes this. 'The solecism *a graffiti*' is 'surprising and distressing', according to a letter in the *Daily Telegraph*. But most English plurals now end with *s*, so the treatment of *graffiti* as singular is in line with the general tidying up process, which has been going on for centuries. Language is not crumbling away. It is maintaining itself efficiently.

The 'infectious disease' idea is the third commonly expressed notion. In an article entitled 'Polluting our language', the writer Douglas Bush expressed a widespread view that we somehow 'catch' changes from those around us, and that we ought to fight such diseases: 'The wholesale spread of corruption may surely be ascribed to mere infection, to the careless, unthinking assimilation of the floating germs which envelop us.' Change is indeed brought about through social contact, so the catching notion is not entirely wrong. But the 'disease' metaphor falls down. People pick up changes because they want to. They want to fit in with social groups, and they adapt their hairstyle, clothes, and language, to those of people they admire, as with the Jocks and Burnouts, teenagers in a suburban high school in Detroit. Jocks were regular guys, who joined in school sports and wanted to conform. Burnouts were rebels who took drugs and behaved unconventionally. The speech of these two groups showed clear differences, with the Jocks imitating the standard adult pattern, but the Burnouts moving away from it.

Adapting to those around is normal human behaviour. In Belfast, in Northern Ireland, a deep-rooted hostility exists between Protestants and Catholics, two religious–ethnic groups which barely talk to one another, and are sometimes in open conflict. Yet when the speech patterns of a group of East Belfast men were compared with those of a group of West Belfast women, both groups showed a tendency to pronounce *grass* as *grawss* at a time when in theory, the two halves of Belfast barely talked to one another. What could have been happening? The mind boggles. Yet the explanation was quite simple. East Belfast men sometimes visited a city-centre store staffed by mainly West Belfast women. It is well known that shop assistants match their speech to that of their customers, and this is what was happening. The shop assistants were then transferring the pronunciation to their friends.

But changes are not random. They take hold only if the language is predisposed to move in a particular direction. Social contact can trigger a change only if it was already likely to happen. The predisposition factor is often overlooked. At any time, in any language, a number of potential change-points exist. Anomalies tend to get smoothed out, as with the pattern-neatening of past tenses and plurals. Human ears and the human vocal tract cause others. Consonants at the end of words are a recurring weak spot in languages, since ends of words are pronounced with less force than beginnings: it's *Kick* not *kiCK*. In British English, *t* at the end of words is eroding, moving from *street* to *stree(t)* with a glottal stop and in the long run, it will probably be *stree*. The change is found in so-called Estuary English – an accent found in south-east England, radiating out from the area around the estuary of the river Thames. Glottal stops are also found in Scotland around Glasgow.

Over time, end-of-word consonants may largely disappear, as has happened in some dialects of Chinese, several Polynesian languages, and nearer at hand, in French and Italian, where most words now end in vowels: *Una bottiglia di vino bianco* 'a bottle of white wine'. Oddly, people who dislike this change often praise languages such as Italian as being 'beautiful' even though many Italian words are derived from Latin ones which once had endings. Italian *vino* 'wine' was once Latin *vinum*: the ending *m* was lost, and the vowel *u* changed to *o*.

Changes are normally triggered by personal contact, as with the Belfast shop assistants, and not via the media. The media are often blamed for change, but their role is indirect. Newspapers can popularize new words such as *bonk, yomp* and *wimp*, even though the words themselves had been around for a long time. *Bonk* 'to copulate', probably an extension of the slang word *bonk* 'to hit', became widely known in 1987 when various tabloid newspapers took an interest in the love life of the tennis player Boris Becker, whom they referred to as 'bonking Becker'. *Yomp* 'to march with heavy equipment over difficult terrain' was a military term used extensively in press reports of the Falklands War in the 1980s. *Wimp* 'a feeble or ineffectual person', usually male, originated in America, but became widely used in England in the 1980s, especially in newspaper reports of politicians who were labelled *wimps*. Radio and television can influence attitudes towards language. These days, they send the sensible but indirect message that it is acceptable to talk in different ways. Prominent entertainers and reporters show that variety is the spice of linguistic life. Their different accents, like their clothes, are a mark of individuality.

Variety is the key to language change. Earlier in the century, an old mutation viewpoint prevailed, that some sounds slowly turned into others, like tadpoles gradually changing into frogs. This is now outmoded. According to a newer view, variant forms arise, each used in a different area or speech style. Then one of the newcomers gets used more and more often, and gradually ousts the older form, like a young cuckoo heaving another bird out of the nest. In some situations, a whole nestful of young cuckoos compete with each other and with older forms. They may squabble for a long time until one wins out.

This process is clearest in the case of vocabulary. It has happened in England with the word *partner* which is now the standard word for life-companion. But at one time numerous words competed, *live-in lover*, *mate*, even *posslq*, an acronym for 'persons of opposite sex sharing living quarters', a strange formation which a few people perhaps remembered because of the rhyme:

There's nothing I wouldn't do
If you would be my *posslq*.

Then the word *partner* gradually pushed the other terms aside. In America, no clear winner has yet emerged, though *significant other* is widely used. The young cuckoo process also happens with pronunciation, as with the *butter* and *bu'er* variants which are competing in British English. They are likely to co-exist, maybe for a longish time. Eventually *bu'er* may well win out. As these examples show, no change can occur without variation, though variation can sometimes exist without change.

Variation in speech is the norm. Our linguistic wardrobe contains a range of speech styles, which we suit to the occasion. Toddlers and tax-inspectors need to be addressed in different ways. Tennis-players, cricketers and taxi-drivers each have their own specialized vocabulary, some words of which are now widely used. Change often happens when one particular variant expands its usage, and spreads across a broader area. But which variants should be used where and when still causes arguments as sharp as barbed-wire, especially as nowadays being 'matey' is often more important than being 'proper', resulting in increasing approval of informal styles of speech, including swearing. This point will be discussed further in chapter 3.

Meanwhile, the tangled web of worries around language shows how little most people know about it. In the next chapter, I will go back to the beginning and discuss the origin of language in the human species. An understanding of how the human language web began can give us insights into language today – and perhaps soothe some worries.

But finally, I'd like to stress again that we need to understand language, not try to control it. Samuel Johnson came to realize this (figure 1.3). In the preface to his dictionary, he said:

> When we see men grow old and die . . ., we laugh at the elixir that promises to prolong life to a thousand years; and with equal justice may the lexicographer be derided, who . . . shall imagine that his dictionary can embalm his language . . . With this hope, however, academies have been instituted to guard the avenues of their languages . . .: but their vigilance and activity have hitherto been in vain; . . . to enchain syllables, and to lash the wind, are equally the undertakings of pride.

1.3 Samuel Johnson and his dictionary

② A web of deceit

The origin of language

Some have held that language was revealed to man by supernatural interference; others, that he spoke naturally and instinctively as a bird sings; others, that language was contrived artificially by men who settled in conclave what arbitrary meaning each sound should bear; others, that the roots of language were sounds having an inherent suitability to express certain ideas, and so on. But . . . like the stories of strange monsters dwelling in the outer regions of the world, they may place themselves on an equal ground of assertion until the time when real knowledge shall come to divide the true from the false.

Edward B. Tylor 'On the origin of language' (1866)

For centuries, ideas about language origin have frothed up like soap bubbles, then burst into nothing. Over 2,000 years ago, the Egyptian king Psammetichus reportedly gave instructions for two new-born children to be brought up in total isolation by a shepherd in a lonely cottage. The king wanted to find out the words they would first utter, which he assumed would reveal the world's oldest race. Two years later, as the shepherd unlocked the cottage-door one day, the children ran up to him with outstretched hands, pronouncing the word *bekos*. Psammetichus discovered with dismay that this was the Phrygian word for 'bread', and reluctantly concluded that the Phrygians predated the Egyptians. But according to John Webb, a seventeenth-century writer, Chinese was the original language of humankind. Happily, it was spoken by Noah and his family in the Ark, he assumed, and so survived the flood. In the mid-nineteenth century, Abbot O'Donnelly, a Frenchman, claimed a 'new and prodigious discovery of the original universal language' supposedly found on an Egyptian obelisk. His translation, he boasted, 'was sufficient to open the eyes of a mole'. But no one listened, he lamented, with his 'words and results being blown away by the wind'.

As one weird idea after another bubbled up, language origin was regarded as a playground for cranks, and the topic was banned in 1866 by the Linguistic Society of Paris, the most prominent linguistic association of the time. And disapproval continued: 'The greater part of what is said and written upon it is mere windy talk', said the linguist William Dwight Whitney in 1893. The origin of language has become a serious field of enquiry only in the last ten years or so, and is the topic of this chapter.

A fresh look at the role of language has led to new ideas about how it all started. Traditionally, humans are regarded as reliable fact-swappers, and conveying information is often claimed to be the primary purpose of language. This view was put forward by philosophers, such as the seventeenth-century thinker John Locke, who stated that language is 'the great conduit, whereby men convey their discoveries, reasonings, and knowledge, from one to another': his conduit metaphor was probably based on his admiration for the pipes which carried London's recently established water supply.

But the conduit idea is misleading. Language is not like a water-pipe. It is good at transferring some types of data, especially negative reports, such as: 'No buses will run on Sunday', or 'The milk hasn't arrived' – provided that the speaker is telling the truth. Yet it is bad at other types, especially spatial information, where instructions such as 'Take the third turning on the right then the fourth on the left' would be much clearer on a map. And as for tying knots, the writer Hilaire Belloc once said: 'If you can describe clearly without a diagram the proper way of making this or that knot, then you are a master of the English tongue.' Perhaps he should have said: 'You will have considerable difficulty describing a knot, however many languages you have mastered.' Language is also bad at conveying pain or emotion. 'There is no language for pain . . . Ouch, ow, oof, gah . . . Pain is its own language', says the novelist Martin Amis. And the paucity of language 'constrains our capacity to communicate the range and subtlety of our emotional responses', points out the psychotherapist Susie Orbach. This patchwork of efficiency and inefficiency is fairly typical of behaviour that is biologically programmed: just as animal teeth have gradually become specialized in the course of evolution, in that rabbits nibble grass but do not crack nuts, similarly, human language has evolved to deal with some things, but not others.

Early human language was probably not a fact-swapping device. Its original role can be uncovered by looking at behaviour which we share with our ape relatives, according to anthropologists. Humans, alongside other primates, are often called social animals. They have firm family ties and also interact strongly at the group level. This social background has promoted two types of behaviour: a fondness for grooming one another, and an ability to make guesses about the mental state of others: intelligent primates can put themselves into one another's shoes, as it were. These abilities tie in with two things language is especially good at: interacting with others, and influencing them.

Humans use language to keep in touch with one another, to weave a web of friendship. Speech takes place at close quarters, and social talking may be a substitute for the friendly grooming found among primates, according to one theory. The 'Hello, how are you, isn't it a nice day?' kind of greeting has even been called 'grooming talking'. Friendly gossip can be thought of as a kind of mutual grooming, in which the participants take it in turns to stroke one another. Traditionally, gossip is associated with women. But it's not just women chatting. Consider a conversation in P. G. Wodehouse's novel *Carry on, Jeeves*:

> 'What ho!' I said.
> 'What ho!' said Motty.
> 'What ho! What ho!'
> 'What ho! What ho! What ho!'

Even if they have nothing to say, humans take it in turns to mouth empty greetings at one another. Such conversational turn-taking starts early in life. Listen to a mother and baby: mother says: 'And how's my little darling today?', then typically waits until the baby coos or burps or otherwise takes its turn before she continues. Such turn-taking may have predated language: mothers and babies have possibly cooed and gurgled at one another for millennia.

Turn-taking is often a kind of ritual: you can frequently guess what the participants are planning to say. If you make an offer: 'Would you like a cup of tea?', you expect that offer to be accepted: 'Thanks, I'd love one.' If you apologize: 'I'm terribly sorry, I spilt some coffee on your carpet', you expect the problem to be minimized: 'O please don't worry, it really doesn't matter.' Similar patterns are found all over the world.

And solidarity talk – vocalizing to strengthen social ties – may extend even further, perhaps including chants before sports matches. The New Zealand rugby team has a joint team-chant known as the *haka*. This may be matched by chimpanzee pant-hoots, which according to some recent research, are male solidarity calls.

Human grooming talking is satirized by the science-fiction writer Douglas Adams. Ford Prefect, a being from another planet, was puzzled by the peculiar human habit

> of continually stating and restating the very obvious, as in 'It's a nice day', or 'You're very tall', or 'So this is it, we're going to die.' His first theory was that if humans didn't keep exercising their lips, their mouths probably seized up. After a few months of

observation, he had come up with a second theory . . .: 'If human beings don't keep exercising their lips, their brains start working.'

But humans don't just verbally scratch each other's backs. They use language to influence and persuade one another. An effective persuader must be able to imagine events from another person's point of view. In fashionable jargon, he or she must have a 'theory of mind'. Without it, persuasion is a hit-and-miss affair.

Animals who possess a theory of mind are good at social manipulation: they can intentionally deceive one another, a skill found among most primate species, though some are better at it than others. Monkeys are fairly poor at it. Baboons and great apes are good at it. Among the great apes, chimpanzees, our close relatives, are extremely skilled deceivers. An infant chimp may scream as if it is being attacked in order to persuade its mother to comfort and feed it. An older chimp may lead others away from hidden food, then double back and scoff the lot by itself. This ability to deceive has been labelled Machiavellian intelligence, after the fifteenth-century Italian who wrote a guide showing how future rulers could manipulate others.

Our ape relatives use deception almost always for selfish reasons. Humans differ, in that deception can be used for good purposes, as well as bad: for reasons of tact, as well as for dishonesty. Humans are not only good deceivers, but also good persuaders and good sympathizers: they can calculate how to influence others, and how to please them. An ability to deceive is therefore an advantage – as long as it is used wisely.

A web of deceit

All this deceit may at first sight seem a long way from language. But a crucial connection exists. The ultimate goal of learning to speak may be lying, or more accurately, a spin-off from lying – the ability to talk convincingly about things which are absent or even non-existent. This property of language, known as displacement, is one of its great strengths. Talking about the past and future is important in any human society, and imaginary events loom large in songs and literature: 'Once upon a time, there were three little pigs', and so on.

A web of deceit, an ability to fib, is therefore crucial to language. This may seem bizarre, since most of us disapprove of lying:

> Matilda told such Dreadful Lies,
> It made one Gasp and Stretch one's Eyes;

said Hilaire Belloc in his *Cautionary tales for children*, in which lying Matilda is burned to death.

Yet even in England, where we pride ourselves on being straightforward, social lying is approved of. Politicians, salespersons, parents, maybe all of us, are 'economical with the truth' when it suits us, and 'little white lies' are an essential component of politeness. Mrs Skewton, a character in Charles Dickens' novel *Dombey and son*, couldn't stop yawning as she was shown round Warwick Castle. But she assured her guide that for her, yawning was a demonstration of delight – a truly tactful lady.

Friendship and deceit are therefore essential prerequisites of language. But they alone were not enough to trigger it.

Human language developed only when these pre-language webs were combined with a unique human feature – a complex sound structure. All primates can hear and discriminate a wide range of sounds, but the ability of non-human primates to produce speech-sounds is limited, for two reasons. First, they cannot easily suppress their own spontaneous calls. 'Ow!' you or I might involuntarily call out, if we trod on a nail. But mostly, humans can opt to remain silent. Other apes find it harder to hold back a wider range of calls, which they spontaneously emit when, for example, they make love or contemplate food. Withholding calls is difficult, though not impossible, as shown by Papoose, a female gorilla who wanted to mate with Titus, a youngish animal, rather than the older dominant male in the group. She and Titus managed to retain secrecy by suppressing normal copulatory calls. In another case, Figan, a chimp who was given some bananas, eventually learned not to make excited calls, bringing other chimps to the scene. But these cases of suppression are unusual enough to have caught the attention of the zoologists studying these animals.

Second, vocal fine-tuning is impossible for other apes. The sounds they make are variable and unclear, partly because they cannot close off the passage to the nose. But in humans, the tongue forms roughly a right angle with the wind-pipe, like an upside-down letter L, and the larynx or voice-box is lower than in chimps. This enables humans to shut off the nasal cavity when they speak, and to make a range of precise and recogniz-able non-nasal sounds.

Human vocal precision is quite odd, by primate standards,

and the human sound system has more in common with bird-song than the grunts of our ape cousins. Birds are capable of precise vocal control, so much so that Lord Monboddo, a Scottish lawyer, claimed in 1773 that we humans learned how to sing and speak from birds, especially cuckoos, ravens and parrots, just as he assumed we discovered how to spin and weave from spiders.

But birds and humans are not copying one another, according to zoologists. Independently, they have each evolved a sound system which shares a number of features. For example, humans have a number of instinctive cries: a baby's scream of pain or yell of hunger is recognizable world-wide. These cries are not real language, which exists alongside, as a separate system, and is acquired as the child matures. Similarly, many birds have a few pre-set calls, such as a call to congregate or a danger cry, as well as more complex songs, whose outline is fixed, but whose finer details often have to be learned.

Language proper is itself double-layered. Single noises are only occasionally meaningful: mostly, the various speech sounds convey coherent messages only when combined into an overlapping chain, like different colours of ice-cream melting into one another. In birdsong also, individual notes are often of little value: the sequence is what matters. In both humans and birds, control of this specialized sound-system is exercised by one half of the brain, normally the left half, and the system is learned relatively early in life. And just as many human languages have dialects, so do some bird species: in California, the white-crowned sparrow has songs so different from area to area, that Californians can supposedly tell where they are in the state by listening to these sparrows.

Of course, the parallels between humans and birds must not be overemphasized, because there are also wide differences: mostly, only male birds sing, and female birds burst into song only if injected with the male hormone testosterone. And differences between the songs of different birds are far greater than the differences between human languages, which are remarkably similar in their overall structure. In addition, human language is an intimate style of communication, compared with birdsong, which unamplified, carries over greater distances – sometimes several kilometres. The record is probably held by the kakapo, a New Zealand flightless parrot, whose sonic booms attract mates from several kilometres away – though humans can sometimes adapt the tones and rhythm of their language to produce long-distance communication, as in the 'talking-drums' of Africa (see figure 2.1). Such adaptations reveal one further unique feature of human language. It can be transferred to other media: drum beats, sign language, or writing.

But the parallels between human language and birdsong are striking. Complex sound systems apparently acquire parallel characteristics. This indicates that both human language and birdsong are the end-product of a long period of evolution. We humans are a zoological curiosity: just as the hoatzin, a weird type of bird, has a stomach somewhat like that of a cow, and a Newfoundland, a weird type of dog, has webbed feet a bit like a duck's, so humans, a weird type of ape, have evolved a

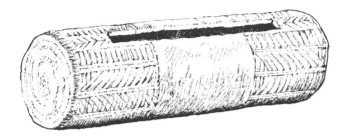

A 'talking drum' reproduces the tones and rhythms of spoken language. Ten or more syllables of 'drum language' may be needed to express unambiguously a meaning that is clearly conveyed in a single syllable of spoken language. Among the Lokele of the Upper Congo, the spoken word for 'dog' is **ngwa**, with one syllable. The drum-language phrase has fourteen, and in translation is 'giant dog, little one that barks **kpei, kpei**'. This long sequence is required to make it clear that what is being described is a dog and not some other item that shares with **ngwa** the properties of being a low-toned one-syllable word. The word for 'goat' is **mbuli**, and is beaten out as a sequence which means 'little goat of the village'. The word for 'banana' is **likondo**. The equivalent drum phrase means literally 'bunch of bananas propped up'.

2.1 Talking drums of Africa

communication system more like that of birds than that of their ape cousins.

Arguments continue about how humans acquired their birdlike skill. Most people assume that language evolved in one geographical region, and then spread outwards, partly because all languages are similar in their basic ground-plan. All languages have nouns, typically words for people and things, and verbs, typically words for actions. These can be combined into longer sequences, such as *Harry snored, Barbara watched a butterfly*. All languages can say who did what to whom, can ask questions, and issue commands. All sentences of any language have syntax, a hidden structure which its speakers can manipulate without apparent effort. On hearing a sentence such as *Uncle Henry ate fifteen bananas*, an English speaker would have no problem in subconsciously realizing that the sentence falls into various chunks, *Uncle Henry, ate, fifteen bananas*, and could re-organize these in a new way: 'Did you say fifteen bananas were eaten by Uncle Henry?' And sentences can potentially go on indefinitely, as suggested by the notice reputedly posted up in a civil servant's office: 'I know you believe that you understand what you think I said. But I am not sure you realize that what you heard is not what I meant.'

Modern humans and human language probably came from one area of the globe, from Africa. Archaeological traces and clues from DNA and blood-groups support this conclusion. One scenario is known as the East Side story. Several hundred thousand years ago, we and our chimp cousins spread across Africa. Then a major earthquake, or 'tectonic event' as it is sometimes called, created the Great Rift Valley, splitting Africa into lush forest to the west and relatively dry savannah to the east. The chimps were left in the tree-filled west. Future humans were stranded in the arid east (see figure 2.2). Their dry savannah became even drier, and they were forced to adapt, or die. One adaptation was meat-eating, as humans learned to supplement their vegetarian diet by scavenging. This possibly promoted brain growth, which may have aided the development of language.

Nature is over-generous in providing pathways along which animals may evolve. Multiple routes are available for exploitation. Evolution is as much a case of suppressing some options, as it is of selecting others. Language may have been a lucky choice out of a range of alternatives. Comments by the poet Robert Frost on his life could well apply to the human race as a whole:

> Two roads diverged in a wood, and I –
> I took the one less travelled by,
> And that has made all the difference.

Once a particular path has been chosen, this constrains future choices, just as leaves which fall off trees cannot leap back on again. Language was a lucky choice which paid off, and has been paying off ever since.

But just how it all got started is still partly a puzzle. Early words could have arrived via several routes. In the last century, three ideas predominated. According to a so-called 'pooh-pooh' theory, language began as cries of emotion: 'ooh! aah! ai! ha!'

33

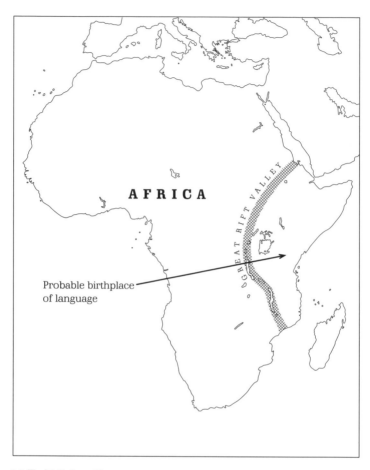

2.2 The birthplace of language

But a 'ding-dong' proposal, that language started by imitating natural sounds, was supported by Charles Darwin. He speculated that an 'unusually wise ape-like animal' may have imitated the growl of a beast of prey, and so informed his fellows of the danger. A 'yo-he-ho' hypothesis, that heaving and hauling gave rise to early words, is the most plausible of these early ideas: the vocal cords were in origin membranes deep in the throat which closed off the lungs, making the rib-cage rigid when some effort is required. The grunt as the air is expelled can be heard in some old sea shanties.

Yet the problem is not so much how sounds arose as how particular sounds came to be used as symbols with firm meanings. The vervet, an agile African monkey with a black face and a long tail, may represent an intermediate phase. Vervets have warning calls which distinguish different types of danger: at a *chutter* they stand on their hind legs and look around for a snake, at a *rraup* they dive into the undergrowth as if hiding from an eagle, and at a *chirp* they climb a tree and look around for a lion or leopard (see figure 2.3). Squirrel monkeys in South America also distinguish between different perils. But these monkey danger calls are not pure naming: they are a cry of fear, a warning to others, and only partially a symbol. Naming for the sake of naming is a major hurdle for animals. The 'naming insight', the realization that things have 'names' is hard for them to grasp – though it comes naturally to humans, as will be discussed in the next chapter.

A stack of single words was probably in common use long before any 'grammar' emerged. Rules, in the sense of recurring

Vervet monkeys have different alarm calls depending on whether the danger is a snake, a leopard or an eagle. Each alarm call brings about a different type of behaviour. At a 'chutter', the other vervets stand on their hind legs and look around for a snake. Other monkey species also have been found to distinguish between types of predator: for example, South American squirrel monkeys have different alarm calls for a threat on the ground and an enemy in the air.

2.3 Vervet danger calls

patterns, could have started in more than one way. Individual
words might have been placed together, much as many children
start off with single words, such as *hi*, *byebye*, *mummy*, *daddy*,
which they later combine in a predictable way, as in *byebye
daddy*, *hi mummy*, and so on. Of course, those who set language going in the first place were unlikely to be babies.

But neatening up was a more likely way for rules to emerge.
Numerous words were placed together randomly and repeti-
tively: *Meat I want, meat want I meat*, for example, perhaps
not unlike the sign sequences of the chimp Nim Chimpsky,
who was taught a language with signs for words. Nim tended to
repeat items. Like most chimps, he was fairly greedy, and his
food anxiety gave rise to many repeated signs: as in *eat me eat,
nut Nim nut, drink eat drink eat*. His longest recorded sign
sequence was:

> give orange me give eat orange me eat orange give me eat orange
> give me you.

The message was clear: Nim wanted an orange.

But for more complex messages, those which go beyond
obvious requests, more structure is needed. In language change
today, optional patterns become habits, then the habits become
obligatory. Our best guess is that something similar happened
at the origin of language. Even Nim Chimpsky showed some
signs of this process. When requesting food, he almost always
put the food word first, as in *grape eat, banana Nim eat, apple
me eat*. And another chimp, Kanzi invented a possible ordering
sequence when he was taught a system involving lexigrams

(picture-words). He indicated first a lexigram for an action, such as *tickle*, *chase*, then he pointed to the person whom he wanted to tickle or chase him.

Human beings also have inbuilt preferences, some of which may have predated language. When humans talk about two items, they prefer to locate the small on the large. They say:

> The cat sat on the mat
> The bird perched on the tree

rather than

> The mat lay under the cat
> The tree stood under the bird

It's part of the human mind-set to envisage the world in this way.

As another preference, all over the world, humans are more likely to say the equivalent of: *Harriet was hit by a cabbage*, rather than *A cabbage hit Harriet*. Animate beings tend to get placed before inanimate things.

Again, humans prefer to put verbs near the objects affected. A sequence *Henry ate an apple*, or *Henry an apple ate* is statistically more likely in the languages of the world than *Ate Henry an apple* – even though this last order is not impossible, being found in Welsh for example.

Many more preferences can be found, and they sometimes clash, which is why all languages are not more similar. But in general: preferences become tendencies, tendencies become habits, and habits become rules. This provides some clues as to why languages do not fly apart in crazy ways: the human mind-set pushes our thoughts in certain directions.

Language possibly neatened itself up with rules only gradually: 'If it all gets too much of a muddle, try a bit of organization' might have been a subconscious maxim – perhaps somewhat like the man who supposedly lost an open umbrella on his untidy desk: this made him decide to tidy it up. Language was probably at first messy and only partially structured, but acquired more and firmer rules as it became more complex. Conventions were needed in order to ensure understanding of who was doing what to whom, and when.

This all led to a more precise type of web, a web of rules. In the next chapter, I will discuss how children born today acquire this rule-web, whose overall structure is preordained.

So after at least fifty thousand years of evolution, the language web is the same the world over in its broad outline. Some nineteenth-century travellers were surprised by this: 'The grammar is precise and somewhat complicated . . .' said a Mr Bell in 1899 about the language of the Miskitu Indians, who live on the north-east coast of South America. He continued: 'It seems strange to find among an uncultivated and uncivilised race rules of grammar as precise and well known as are used by the most cultivated nations of Europe . . . How is this to be explained?'

❸ Building the web

Acquiring language

'Darling? Come and sit on my lap
... And read a book. Come and sit
on Daddy's lap. There's a good boy
... What's that? What's that,
darling?'
    'Dick'.
    'Stick. Very good. Ssssstick ...
Marmaduke, you're a genius.
What's that? ... Don't do that
darling. Ow ...'
    As Guy lent forward to give a
farewell kiss to the increasingly
restless child – Marmaduke caught
him with a reverse headbutt. It was
probably at least semi-accidental.

Martin Amis London Fields (1989)

ET, the well-known Extra-Terrestrial, learnt human language fast: 'His ear-flap opened and he listened intently ... His ... circuits buzzed, assimilating, synthesizing ... Thus inspired, the language centre of his marvellous brain came fully on ...' Yet ET's magical ability is almost matched by that of human children. As the American statesman Benjamin Franklin once said: 'Teach your child to hold his tongue; he'll learn fast enough to speak.'

The language web

Children talk so readily because they instinctively know in advance what languages are like. As in a spider's web, the outline is preprogrammed, and the network is built up in a pre-ordained sequence. The predictable way in which the language web develops is the topic of this chapter, including how adults can help, or sometimes even slow down a child's progress.

Language has a biologically organized schedule (see figure 3.1). Children everywhere follow a similar pattern. In their first few weeks, babies mostly cry. As Ronald Knox once said: 'A loud noise at one end, and no sense of responsibility at the other.' Crying exercises the lungs and vocal cords. But crying may once have had a further evolutionary purpose. Yelling babies may have reminded parents that their offspring exist: deaf ringdoves forget about their existing brood, and go off and start another.

From six weeks onwards, infants *coo* or even *mew* according to some older accounts, which sometimes compared these early gurgles to the twittering of birds. From around six months, babies babble language-like sounds. 'He called me mummy' is a typical squawk of a delighted new parent, as a child exercises its mouth with the sequence *ma-ma-ma* or *da-da-da*. Over-interpretation by parents is why the words *mama*, *papa* and *dada* are found all over the world for 'mother' and 'father', closely followed by *kaka* for 'excrement'.

A widespread myth circulates, that infants burble all sounds of every language. This is untrue, the range is in fact rather limited. The myth arose partly because some early researchers found it hard to distinguish early infant gurgles,

From WEEK 0 Crying

WEEK 6 Cooing (goo-goo)

WEEK 6 Babbling (ma-ma)

WEEK 8 Intonation patterns

MONTH 12 Single words

MONTH 18 Two-word utterances

YEAR 2 Word endings

YEAR 2½ Negatives

YEAR 2¼ Questions

YEAR 5 Complex constructions

YEAR 10 Mature speech patterns

3.1 Typical speech timetable for English-speaking child

and partly because children do indeed produce some sounds not found in the language they are learning. But a babbling drift takes place, in which children gradually veer towards the sounds found in their own language: Chinese babies are reported to babble single syllables with different tones.

Single words 'Oo! Da!' are produced from around the age of a year. Parents often play naming games with youngsters: they point to a black fluffy blob in a book and say 'cat'. Little Bobby or Suzy imitates, saying maybe *ga*. The discovery that *ga* is a name for the dark splodge comes later. Children do not at first realize that sounds can be labels for things. Early words are tied strongly to a location, and often relate to a whole scene. A word *da* for a toy duck might be for one particular duck as it floats in a particular bath. Only later will *da* be used for a duck away from the bath, and later still extended to all ducks, and maybe swans, geese – and even toy boats.

The naming insight, the discovery that things have names, is a major leap forward. Children pass this milestone at various times, typically before the age of eighteen months. Parents don't usually notice it, it seems so normal, because adults expect things to have names. But for youngsters, the naming discovery can be a shock, as shown by occasional children who come to it late. Helen Keller was deaf and blind from the age of two. Then, when she was six, her teacher held her hand under a flow of water, and spelled out the word w-a-t-e-r on the other. She later wrote: 'Somehow the mystery of language was revealed to me. I knew then that "w-a-t-e-r" meant the wonderful cool something that was flowing over my hand. That living word awakened my soul . . ., set it free! . . . Everything had a name, . . . every object which I touched seemed to quiver with life.'

The naming insight is followed by a 'naming explosion'. Names come popping out of children like stars out of fireworks. This eruption in vocabulary leads to word combinations, *mummy push, daddy car* and so on. Some phrases are novel, as *byebye sock, allgone kitty*, which are unlikely to have been copied from adults. Recurring patterns are found as with *sand toe*, 'I've got sand in my toes', *sand eye* 'I've got sand in my eye', and *sand hair* 'I've got sand in my hair'. The parents were probably too busy mopping the sand off this child to admire the consistency of its language rules.

Youngsters look for regularities in language, as shown by the *wug*-test, devised by Jean Berko Gleason in the 1950s. 'Here is a wug', she said, showing a picture of a bird-like creature. Then she showed two of them: 'Now there are two . . .' 'Wugs' responded children from a very young age.

Children do not always get it right first time. Two-year-old Sophie learned the words *broken, fallen* and *taken*. She wrongly concluded that English past tenses end in *-en*. She then invented a whole range of new past tense forms, such as *boughten, builden, riden, getten, cutten, wanten, touchen, maden, tippen,* as in 'me tippen that over'. Sophie gradually dropped these *-en* forms – probably when she discovered the normal past tense for each verb. Children dislike finding two words which mean exactly the same thing, and usually drop one of them.

By the age of three, children utter long sentences, though some things, such as pronouns, still cause problems. Three-year-old Adam said his doll 'shuts she's eyes', instead of 'shuts her eyes'.

At around three and a half, children talk freely. By this time, they have acquired most of the constructions used by adults. This is true of monolingual children, and also bilingual ones. A few gaps still exist for all children up to the age of around ten, and word-learning goes on throughout life.

This predictable sequence of events is typical of biologically scheduled behaviour, as pointed out by Eric Lenneberg, a pioneer in this field. His book *Biological foundations of language*, published in 1967, was a major landmark. Before then, natural behaviour, such as seals swimming, was usually separated from nurtured or learned behaviour, as when seals can be taught to jump through hoops.

Lenneberg showed that this divide is over simple. Most natural behaviour requires some learning: pigeons naturally fly, but they have to spend time learning how to stay in the air. Conversely, learning would be impossible if it did not build on natural talents: pigeons can be trained to distinguish between letters of the alphabet, but only because they already have acute eyesight.

Language is an example of maturationally controlled behaviour, Lenneberg pointed out, behaviour which is pre-programmed to emerge at a particular stage in an individual's life, provided the surrounding environment is normal. Walking and sexual behaviour are other examples. Such behaviour emerges before it is critically needed, yet cannot be forced to appear before it is scheduled. Some learning is required, but the learning cannot be significantly speeded up by coaching. No external event or conscious decision causes it, and a regular sequence of milestones can be charted.

An ability to cope with language structure is largely separate from general intelligence. In recent years, several so-called 'cocktail party chatterers' have been discovered – children who have a non-verbal IQ so low that they may not even know their own age, but who speak fluently. As at cocktail parties, they talk for the sake of talking, and their speech may not make sense. Take Laura, an American teenager: 'I was sixteen last year, and now I'm nineteen this year' or 'It was no regular school, it was just good old no buses.' Such chatterbox children are not just repeating set phrases, because they make grammatical mistakes which they are unlikely to have heard, as in Laura's statement that 'Three tickets were gave out by a police last year.'

Just as bees learn fast to distinguish flowers from, say, balloons or bus-stops, so human children are preset by nature to pick out natural language sounds: they do not get distracted by barking dogs or quacking ducks. Their learning is innately guided (see figure 3.2). Inbuilt signposts direct youngsters, so they instinctively pay attention to certain linguistic features, such as stressed vowels and word order. Children's main task is to discover which of these features have priority in the language or languages they are acquiring, just as bees have to learn whether to look for heather, roses or lilies.

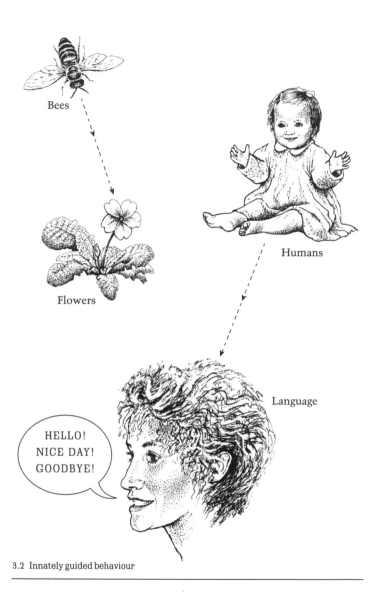

Bees

Flowers

Humans

Language

HELLO!
NICE DAY!
GOODBYE!

3.2 Innately guided behaviour

Building the web

A biological time-clock ordains the sequence in which the language web is woven, though not the exact dates. But nobody is quite sure when the clock starts ticking, and when it stops. According to Lenneberg, humans are scheduled to acquire language within a critical period between the ages of two and thirteen, a time preordained by human nature. After that, the acquisition of language was difficult, he claimed, maybe impossible.

Lenneberg turns out to be partially wrong and partially right. He is wrong about the starting-point. Language acquisition begins well before the age of two. Babies only a few days old can pick out their own language, according to some research by Jacques Mehler and his colleagues in Paris. The infants responded to French with increased sucking movements, a standard reaction to sounds which interested them. But they did not display the same reaction to other languages. So infants still in the womb may become accustomed to the rhythms of the language spoken around them.

And language development does not come to a shuddering halt at adolescence, as Lenneberg assumed: vocabulary even undergoes a spurt at this time. So the idea of a fixed critical period is now disputed.

Yet most people find it easier to learn languages when they are young – so a sensitive period may exist, a time early in life when acquiring language is easiest, and which tails off gradually, though never entirely.

A 'natural sieve' hypothesis is one idea put forward to explain this. Very young children may extract only certain limited features from what they hear, and may automatically filter out many complexities. Later learners may have lost this inbuilt filter, and be less able to cope as everything pounds in on them simultaneously. A 'tuning-in' hypothesis is another possibility. At each age, a child is naturally attuned to some particular aspect of language. Infants may be tuned in to the sounds, older children to the syntax, and from around ten onwards, the vocabulary becomes a major concern. Selective attention of this type fits in well with what we know about biologically programmed behaviour.

The outlines of the language web are therefore preordained. Acquiring language involves weaving in the network details of one's own native tongue, with particular portions scheduled to be filled in at particular ages.

Japanese, Welsh or Samoan – children handle all languages with equal efficiency. The American linguist Noam Chomsky has suggested that children might be innately endowed with advance information on the main ways in which languages can vary. So children may have to discover whether they are dealing with an English-type language, which puts verbs in front of its objects, or a Turkish-type one which does the reverse. Once a decision is made, the child metaphorically 'sets a switch', with multiple repercussions. If, as in English, a language has verbs before its objects, as in *climb the tree*, then it will also probably have prepositions before nouns as in *up the tree*. A language such as Hindi or Turkish would have the reverse, and say, as it were, *the tree climb*, and *the tree up*. It is as if the child was sitting in a linguistic bath, and watching which way water swirled down the plughole, clockwise or anti-clockwise. Once the youngster had found this out, then it would automatically know the linguistic equivalent of whether it was in the northern or southern hemisphere, and whether days got warmer to the north or to the south. In technical terminology, children 'set parameters', a mathematical term for a fixed property whose values vary (see figure 3.3).

Chomsky makes acquiring language sound like turning on a light, more instantaneous than it really is. But his theory rightly emphasizes that any language holds together in a network of implications. If a language has one type of construction, others are predictable from it.

But natural web-spinning can be both helped and sometimes hindered by the speech of those around. Early research talked of motherese, mother's speech. This left out fathers and friends, so caretaker speech became the fashionable term, later amended to caregiver speech, and in academic publications, to CDS 'child directed speech'. I'll leave it at caregivers. Another term 'baby-talk' is best avoided, because it usually refers to *gee-gee*, *puff-puff*, *moo-cow*-type words, so puzzlingly widespread in England when talking to babies or sending Valentines.

Caregiver speech can be odd. Some parents are more concerned with truth than with language. The ill-formed 'Daddy hat on' might meet with approval, 'Yes, that's right', if daddy was wearing a hat. But the well-formed 'Daddy's got a hat on' might meet with disapproval, 'No, that's wrong', if daddy wasn't wearing a hat. You might expect children to grow up telling the truth, but speaking ungrammatically, as some early researchers pointed out. In fact, the opposite happens.

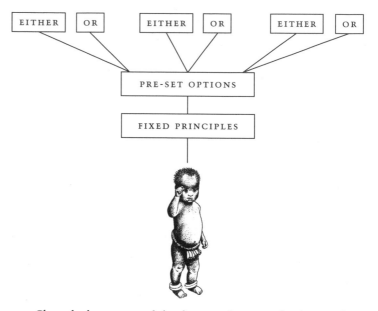

Chomsky has suggested that language has some fixed principles which children instinctively know. In addition, he has proposed that language has a number of pre-set 'either–or' options, and children must discover which options have been selected by their own language. They then metaphorically 'set a switch' which will have multiple repercussions. In technical terminology, Chomsky speaks of 'setting parameters'. A parameter is a fixed property with variable settings: for example, temperature is a parameter of the atmosphere, sweetness is a parameter of wine. In languages in which word order is important, a child might be pre-set to notice if objects come after verbs, as in English *I want an apple*, or before verbs, as in Turkish *elmayı*, 'apple want-I'. This is likely to tie in with whether a language has prepositions, as in *from the house*, or postpositions, as in Turkish *evdan*, 'house-from'.

3.3 Chomsky's switch-setting

Building the web

Parents also reportedly care about etiquette: 'Say please', or they pick on swear words: 'Don't let me hear you say that word again', or they notice occasional pronunciation problems : 'Say Trisha, not Twisha.' If they do pick on language formation, it's often verb endings: this may be useful, if the child is tuned in at that time to learning these. If not, the correction is likely to be ignored. One much-quoted conversation was about baby rabbits:

> 'My teacher holded the baby rabbits, and we patted them', said the child.
> 'Would you say she held them tightly?' asked mother
> 'Oh no, she holded them loosely', replied her daughter.

At best, a sensitive parent provides support, by being aware of structures to which the child is attuned. Mostly, parents muddle along, sometimes getting it right, sometimes wrong. At worst, a grumbling tone of voice can sap confidence: a child may realize that something is wrong, but not always know what. Only talk directly addressed to the youngster has an effect. Vincent, a hearing child born to deaf parents, learned to communicate with sign language. He himself could hear, and he used to sit in front of the television, and watch the pictures with fascination. But apparently, he did not pay any attention to the sounds. He did not start to speak until he went to school, where people talked to him. And a recent survey in Manchester found that television can delay speech development even in some normal children: they are riveted by the colours and flashing lights, and tune out the sounds.

The language web

But even with face-to-face contact, the young learner sets the agenda. Clear, varied utterances directly addressed to the youngster are the silken strands out of which the child builds the language web. Caregiver speech is extra-useful when the same words come in more than once in different ways. Many parents do this naturally: 'Now Patsy, where did you get that knife? Give the knife to mummy. Give mummy the knife. There's a good girl.'

The talk has to grab the child's attention. Joint enterprises are all important. Research published around ten years ago showed that parents found it easier to talk to girls, mainly because they involved them more often in domestic chores: 'Come and help mummy with the potatoes', mothers tended to say to their daughters. But 'Go outside and play football', they commanded their sons. Not surprisingly, some families ended up with chattering potato-peeling girls, and tongue-tied football-kicking boys. This was one reason why girls were often a step ahead of boys in their language, it was suggested. Hopefully, this imbalance is being corrected, with both sexes now equally involved in chores, and perhaps equally acquiring language.

But if people talk to them, all children respond well. They enjoy pit-patting the conversational ball backwards and for-wards. 'Put on your coat', said father. 'Why?' asked junior. 'Because we're going out.' 'Why?' 'Because we're going to buy some dinner.' 'Why?' 'Because we have to eat.' 'Why?' At this point, father realized junior was not interested in the answers, but was treating the conversation as a game, which he wanted his father to go on playing.

Building the web

So children build the language web by extracting what they need from the talk they hear around them. Most are efficient chatterers long before they go to school. But they still need to learn which type of speech to use when – so-called 'communicative competence'. In linguistic terminology, different registers suit different occasions. Babies and bank managers must be addressed in different ways, just as different clothes are required for the beach and a wedding. A doctor speaking to another doctor might talk about a *circumorbital haematoma*, but to a schoolboy, it would be a *black eye*.

The language web, then, has been mostly acquired by children by around the age of thirteen, apart from the mixing and matching of language styles, and also vocabulary, which will be the topic of the next chapter.

You might expect parents to cheer as their offspring become competent language users, and give them, say, a reward of a telephone on their thirteenth birthday. But the acquisition story is not yet over. At this age, language suddenly becomes a mudslinging match between generations. Teenagers want to talk like their pals, but parents disapprove. A father was shocked when his daughter informed him that she did not dare talk in her 'posh' home voice at school; she would lose her friends.

Teenage stroppiness is partly to blame, with predictable kicks at convention – though this is normally a temporary phase. Teenagers' language usually gets less extreme as they approach adult life.

But changing speech styles also tangle people up. These

days, formal speech, like a top hat, is used on fewer occasions. Informal speech, like an open-necked shirt, is felt to be friendlier. In this easy-going atmosphere, being 'proper' is often regarded as less important than being 'matey'.

Matiness and casualness are sometimes emphasized by swearing. Swearwords swarm like bees in some recent literature, and buzz about freely in conversation. Yet today's swearwords are undergoing a bleaching process, a fading of meaning that happens in all semantic change. In the last century, oaths using the name of God were widely disapproved of. Then they gradually lost their power to shock. These days, f-words (sexual swearing) and s-words (excrement-swearing) no longer horrify so many people. Their meaning has weakened as the original connection with sex and excrement fades.

But the war of words between the generations is also entwined with the usual cobweb of worries which surround language change. Parents want their offspring to use so-called Standard English. What exactly they mean by this is a question which has long ensnared people in its sticky and dusty threads. The word 'standard' is ambiguous: it can mean either a value which has to be met, as in 'a high standard', or it can mean uniform practice, as in 'standard behaviour'.

These two meanings of standard have long been confused. For example, in 1836, a treatise which offered 'principles of Remedy for Defects of Utterance', commented that 'the common standard dialect is that in which all marks of a particular place of birth and residence are lost and nothing appears to indicate any other habits of intercourse than with the well-bred and well-informed, wherever they may be found'.

So Standard English came to be thought of as the speech of the educated. This was often assumed to be the language of Oxford, so-called Oxford English, and of the most expensive fee-paying schools (known in England as 'public schools'). So the word 'standard' moved from meaning general usage to that of a specific group to be emulated.

But it's important to distinguish between accent, which describes pronunciation, and dialect, which involves grammar. Spoken Standard English is not an accent – as pointed out in a recent survey commissioned by the National Curriculum Council (a body which sets up school curricula in Great Britain). Pronunciation has always varied, and Standard English includes a variety of accents. Different accents are a sign of identity, a badge of one's area. They are a problem only if they are hard to understand. Meanwhile, the grammar of English is fairly similar across the British Isles. Standard spoken English is usually defined as the grammatical forms used in formal public contexts, and they do not vary very much.

But language is always changing, and a few fluctuating forms cause a disproportionate amount of anxiety. The phrase *for you and I*, in place of the presumed 'correct' form, *for you and me*, came out top of the complaints in letters written to the BBC about language. Yet several well-known figures have used it in public quite recently, including Oxford-educated Lady Thatcher, who commented that 'It's not for you and I to condemn the state of the Malawi economy.' A surprising mismatch exists

between what people condemn and the condemned forms they use without noticing. Perhaps the next generation will shake itself free of this cobweb of pseudo-worries.

As this chapter has pointed out, the language web, like a spider's web, is woven in a preordained way. As with spiders, time and effort have to go into the weaving process. But humans, unlike spiders, can think about the webs they have woven. This sometimes gives rise to a superfluous cobweb of worries. Ideally, the final layers of a child's web-building would be supplemented by two extra, conscious strands: tolerance of minor variations and an interest in each other's speech.

In Bernard Shaw's play *Pygmalion*, first performed in 1916, the character Henry Higgins refers to the flower-seller Eliza Doolittle as a 'squashed cabbage leaf', complaining that 'a woman who utters such depressing and disgusting sounds has no right to be anywhere, no right to live'. This narrow-minded view is luckily disappearing. Increasingly, people are beginning to realize that variety is the spice of linguistic life. In John Agard's poem, 'Listen Mr Oxford don', the West Indian speaker claims to be bashing up the language:

> Listen Mr Oxford don
> I'm a man on de run
> and a man on de run
> is a dangerous one
>
> I ent have no gun
> I ent have no knife
> but mugging de Queen's English
> is the story of my life

Building the web

I dont need no axe
To split/ up yu syntax
I dont need no hammer
to mash/ up yu grammar

I'm not a violent man Mr Oxford don
I only armed with mih human breath
but human breath
is a dangerous weapon.

But he's not blowing the Queen's English down, nor is he
breathing germs over it. Quite the contrary. With his skilled
word-weaving, he's breathing extra life into the language.

❹ A web of words

Remembering words

> We open our mouths and out flow words whose ancestries we do not even know. We are walking lexicons ... We carry a museum inside our heads ... I find this miraculous. I never cease to wonder at it.
>
> I have put my faith in language – hence the panic when a simple word eludes me ... I control the world as long as I can name it.
>
> **Penelope Lively** Moon Tiger (1987)

Dean Farrar, a respected nineteenth-century intellectual, once eavesdropped on some apple-pickers: 'I once listened for a long time to the conversation of three peasants who were gathering apples among the boughs of an orchard, and as far as I could conjecture, the whole number of words they used did not exceed a hundred', he guessed. They managed with this low number, he suggested, because 'the same coarse expletives recurred with a horrible frequency in the place of every single part of speech'. Dean Farrar, like numerous others, apparently grossly underestimated the number of words used and known by native speakers of English.

The language web

Words are the topic of this chapter. *The language web* is the title of this whole book, and the human wordstore with its multitude of links is perhaps the most truly weblike of all aspects of language – even though up till recently, both the size and importance of the internal dictionary, or mental lexicon, have been underestimated.

A false but popular view is that the size of a person's lexicon is about two-thirds of Shakespeare's vocabulary, whose plays contain around 30,000 different words. But far more words exist now than in Shakespeare's time, and many speakers probably know twice as many as he did.

An educated native speaker of English knows at least 50,000 words, according to our best guesstimates. The word 'know' refers to 'potentially active vocabulary', that is, words which could be used spontaneously, even though words such as *igloo*, *gladioli*, or *trombone*, might occur only occasionally.

Humans mop up words like sponges. By the age of five, most English-speaking children can actively use around 3,000 words, and more are added fast, often quite long and complex ones. This total rises to 20,000 around the age of thirteen, and to 50,000 or more by the age of about twenty. These figures have been arrived at by tests on the proportion of words known in various dictionaries. A typical university student can use the equivalent of two-thirds of the *Concise Oxford Dictionary*, which claims to contain around 75,000 entries – though most people also know dozens of quite specialized words which do not always find their way into dictionaries, such as chemists who know the chemical elements.

A web of words

Averaging it out, between the ages of five and twenty, a native English speaker acquires more than ten words a day, that is more than 300 a month, and well over 3,000 a year – though the words are unlikely to be acquired at a smooth rate. This far surpasses the achievements of those few chimpanzees who have been taught so-called 'words' via signs or pictures: their total rarely reaches 500, in spite of intensive coaching. As one researcher concluded: 'The only way to begin to account for the child's wizardry as a word learner, given the sheer weight of how much there is to be learned, is to grant that the child brings a great deal to the "original word game".' Word learning ability is clearly inbuilt in humans.

At one time, learning words was thought to be like beach-combing – strolling along the shoreline, picking up different-shaped pebbles and shells, which were then stacked up in a mental museum. This is still the view taken by some language learners, as in Hanif Kureshi's novel *The Buddha of suburbia*, which described an immigrant keen to get accepted:

> Dad . . . always carried a tiny blue dictionary with him . . . making sure to learn a new word every day. At the weekends I'd test him on the meaning of *analeptic*, *frutescent*, *polycephalus*, and *orgulous*. He'd . . . say, 'You never know when you might need a heavyweight word to impress an Englishman.'

But words are not separate pebbles. They are woven into a complex web whose multiple links enable humans to remember and find so many words so quickly.

At a first glance, words are like coins with two sides, meaning on the one side, and sounds on the other. These

63

two sides can get detached. Sometimes, the meaning gets linked to the wrong sounds: Prince Edward, in a television interview about his old school, said: 'It is difficult to use *capital punishment* in any institution. A beating is very valuable – it shows people you have come to the end of your tether.' The prince did not plan to behead his school chums. He'd made a speech error, a slip of the tongue, and said *capital punishment* when he meant 'corporal punishment'. At other times, people know the meaning of the word they want, but cannot think of the sounds, which they are sure are 'on the tip of their tongue'. They are just out of reach, like a submerged dream that floats under the surface of memory.

Word meaning is the side of the coin people often think about first, though humans cannot usually explain the meanings of the tens of thousands of words they use. Defining words like a dictionary is a technical skill which mostly only lexicographers acquire.

A view that words have fixed, precise meanings is an old one which goes back at least to the Greek philosopher Aristotle in the fourth century BC, and it is still found today. According to the novelist Evelyn Waugh, 'words have basic inalienable meanings, departure from which is either conscious metaphor or inexcusable vulgarity'. Traditionally, a word is viewed as a cake, with a set recipe, whose ingredients can be ticked off on a list, sometimes called a 'checklist' view of meaning.

But the checklist idea works only occasionally, mainly for technical terms such as *square* which is 'a closed flat figure, with four sides of equal length, and all interior angles equal'.

It works also for some consciously invented meanings, as in
a bureaucratic definition of a cow: 'A cow is a female bovine
animal which has borne a calf, or has, in the opinion of the
Minister, been brought into a herd to replace one which
has borne a calf.'

But in most cases, woolly boundaries and fuzzy edges are
the norm. Word meanings are like stretchy pullovers, whose
outline contour is visible, but whose detailed shape varies with
use: 'The proper meaning of a word . . . is never something upon
which the word sits like a gull on a stone; it is something over
which the word hovers like a gull over a ship's stern', noted
one literary critic.

The elusive nature of word meaning has been discussed for
quite a long time. Nearly forty years ago, the philosopher
Ludwig Wittgenstein pointed out the 'family resemblance'
phenomenon, using the word *game* as an example. Like
members of a family, every game has similarities with some
other game: ring-a-roses and tennis involve physical activity,
tennis and chess require a winner, chess and patience are
normally played indoors, and so on – but no one factor links
them all. More than twenty years ago, the sociolinguist William
Labov drew attention to the 'fuzzy edges' problem, by asking
people to name various containers. They not only disagreed
with one another over bowls, cups and vases, but were inconsistent from day to day. Certain shapes were clear instances of
particular containers, but others varied: something might be
a bowl when full of potatoes, but a vase when it held flowers.

A possible solution to all this fuzziness was proposed in the mid-1970s by a psychologist, Eleanor Rosch. Humans do not rank all members of a category equally, she pointed out. They judge some to be very good examples, and others less so. So robins and blackbirds are very good birds, which she labelled prototypes. Canaries and doves are less good birds, owls and ducks are bad birds, and a penguin is a very bad bird indeed (see figure 4.1). People analyse the characteristics of the best bird, the prototype, and allow anything which sufficiently resembles it to belong to the category 'bird'. This explains how humans deal with oddities, why ostriches, emus and one-legged albino blackbirds can be accepted as birds.

But children take time to discover adult prototypes. One small girl latched on to a crescent moon as her prototypical moon. She then labelled anything which was crescent shaped and shiny as *moon*, including curved cow-horns, a slice of lemon and a shiny green leaf. For another child, a *rah-rah* began as something dead and bloody which the cat brought in, maybe from the noise made by the animal as it chewed its catch. She then applied the word to her own blood-smeared cuts and bruises, and later to red cherries in ice-cream.

Adult-style ranking may take a long time to emerge. Eleven-year-olds were inconsistent when asked to select the 'best examples' of a category. Older children tended to give a top ranking to items which were important to them: they gave high priority to parrots among birds, because they found them eye-catching, and to potatoes among vegetables because they liked potato chips.

In different cultures, some unexpected differences some-

Good

Bad

Robin Blackbird Duck Owl Emu Penguin

4.1 Good birds and bad birds

times surface. English speakers expect vehicles to have wheels, and regard cars and buses as the best examples. French speakers are less fussy about the wheels, and some accept even skis and lifts as examples of *un véhicule*, 'a vehicle'. Several Italian teachers of English judged that a goose was not a bird, on the grounds that it was a fowl, and that a walnut was a fruit – a dried fruit. And some Swedish teachers of English denied that berries could be fruits. They had all been influenced by their own language, even though they were unaware of this.

But the human word-web involves much more than a set of prototypes. The web is multidimensional. Each word is an intersection point at which numerous strands meet. Some of these linking threads can be identified by 'slips of the tongue', when people accidentally substitute one word for another. 'Do you have a *refrigerator* in your car?' someone asked me. They meant 'air conditioner', showing that names for different cooling mechanisms were linked in their mind. Strong ties exist between words within the same domain of meaning, so *brother* may get substituted for 'sister', *aunt* for 'niece', *tomorrow* for 'yesterday', and so on. Sigmund Freud, incidentally, suggested that word substitutions had some deeper significance, as when the Austrian President declared a meeting of parliament *closed*, when he meant 'opened'. Freud comments: 'No doubt . . . the President secretly *wished* he was in a position to close the sitting.' But this seems over-imaginative. Perhaps the words *close* and *open* are just tightly linked in the mind, and some distraction caused the President to pronounce the wrong one.

Patients with brain-damage sometimes provide further

evidence of word links. A stroke victim may look at a lemon and name it *apple* or *orange*. The word-name has not necessarily disappeared from memory. Instead, closely connected words may have become confused, just as normal speakers cannot always remember which is which among different breeds of dog or makes of car.

How these word-clusters form in people's minds has long been a puzzle. But the answer may be quite simple. Words which can replace one another in a sentence structure often occur together, as *orange* and *lemon*: '*Oranges* and *lemons* say the bells of St Clements'. 'Roses are *red*, violets are *blue*'. '*Girls* and *boys* come out to play', '*Parsley, sage, rosemary and thyme*'.

Even antonyms, opposites, are probably learned because they tend to occur near one another: 'Don't mix *clean* clothes with *dirty* ones', 'You'll have to take the *rough* with the *smooth*', 'She doesn't know if she *loves* him or *hates* him', and so on.

And people often use a couple of words from the same domain to avoid using a more general, technical term, which covers them both. They talk about *brothers and sisters* not 'siblings', *rain and snow* rather than 'precipitation', 'Please put the *knives and forks* on the table' is more usual than 'cutlery', which is a fairly formal term: 'You'll find the cutlery on the fourth floor, madam.' In some cases, a superordinate term does not even exist. What are baths and basins? Are they bathroom fixtures? or sanitary fitments? What are coughs and sneezes? Are these 'noises indicating respiratory distress'? And what about tin-openers and cork-screws which are sometimes confused in slips of the tongue? No single English term covers 'kitchen gadgets for opening things'.

Noticing which words occur together is a natural human talent, the key to sounding like a native speaker. People who grow up speaking British English do not talk about *rank butter* or *rancid eggs* or *rotten weeds*. They reliably refer to *rancid butter*, *rotten eggs*, and *rank weeds*, even though *rancid*, *rank* and *rotten* tend to have overlapping definitions in dictionaries.

Similarly, with *chase* and *pursue*: English speakers use them with different objects, even though they might not consciously realize it. We chase runaway horses, burglars, balls and other physical things, as in: 'More frigging football! Bunch of tarts going round a field chasing a ball!' But we pursue abstract ideas, aims, targets, and policies, as in: 'We need to take the initiative in pursuing a strategy for employment and growth.' So footballs are not normally pursued, nor are targets chased, even though the meaning 'follow after' is given for both *chase* and *pursue* in some dictionaries (see figure 4.2).

And humans learn how to handle new words by paying attention to the other words around, as with *wimp* . This word is widely used, but it has crept into dictionaries only recently, so must have been learned some other way. In a survey of *wimp*-words in newspapers, over 80 per cent were accompanied by clues to its meaning, that of a feeble male:

He *hates wimps*, and *needs strong people*.
You were *a hunk if you drove a Mustang, a wimp if you drove anything else*.
He was *a go-getter, a doer, not some depressed wimp*.

FOLLOW
AFTER (CONCRETE)

JOURNEY
ALONG A PATH (ABSTRACT)

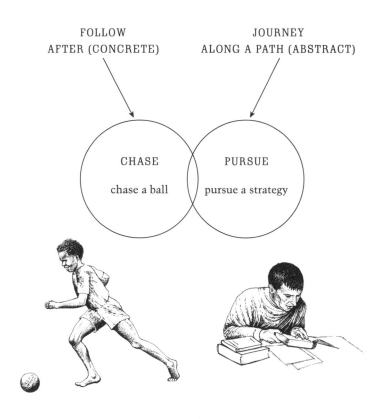

CHASE

chase a ball

PURSUE

pursue a strategy

4.2 Chase vs pursue

And so on.

Humans, then, are supersensitive to words which occur together. Sensitivity to surrounding words is now thought to be the key to learning grammatical rules. Verbs especially are the maypole around which a sentence revolves, and they determine its structure: for example, you have to *put* something somewhere, as *Herbert put the jellyfish in the bath.* You cannot say simply **Herbert put the jellyfish.* The sentence structure must have been picked up by listening to the words around.

But words do not only have meaning links, they also have a sound structure. Information about how humans retrieve word sounds comes from malapropisms, similar sounding words which get confused, as in 'He told a funny *antidote*', for 'He told a funny anecdote'. Mrs Malaprop, the character in Sheridan's play *The Rivals*, said things such as 'as angry as an *allegory* on the banks of the Nile', when she meant 'alligator'. With real adults, a bathtub effect is found. The word is like a person submerged in a bath, their head and feet out of the water, with the head further out than the feet. People get the beginnings of words right, after that the ends, and the middle not very well, as in *transcendental medication* for 'transcendental meditation'. 'It's a policy I regard as *indispensable*', said a government spokesman. He actually meant 'indefensible'. And 'You keep new born chicks warm in an *incinerator*', proclaimed a lecturer: she had meant to say 'incubator'. People also remember the word rhythm and stressed vowel most of the time, though not as well as the beginnings and ends. Numerous similar words are distinguished fast mostly by their different beginnings, as with *ability* and *debility*, or *virility* and *sterility*.

Children, on the other hand, are better than adults at word rhythm, and not so good at word beginnings, as in: 'Daddy, please will you buy me an ice-cream *toilet*' for 'ice-cream cornet', and 'the lion and the *leprechaun*' for 'the lion and the unicorn', *gandigoose* for 'bandicoot', and *marmadillo* for 'armadillo'. They eventually shift over to an adult-like system, partly because they learn to read, and partly because they discover that word beginnings provide a faster way to find words.

Of course, humans do not just remember old words, they also coin new ones. A *dead-cat bounce* is a 'temporary and deceptive share recovery before a final crash', *greenism* is 'commitment to preserving the environment', *middlescence* comes between adolescence and senescence, and a *magaholic* is an insatiable magazine reader – to take a few relatively recent examples.

Most new words simply disappear, like raindrops falling and soaking into the ground. Only a few get caught in the bucket of public attention, and make their way into dictionaries. As an eighteenth-century writer, James Bramston, expressed it:

> Like South Sea stock, expressions rise and fall.
> King Edward's words are now no words at all.

Coining words begins early. Young children easily make up new words, but many of them are odd by adult standards. 'I am *souping*', said a three-year-old, while eating soup. Even eleven- and twelve-year-olds make a lot of odd guesses. For example, a group was asked: 'Suppose there was an insect called a *wug*, what would be a good word for a very small *wug*?' *Woggle*, *wuggable*, and *wugtugbug* were among the suggestions made. But adult type responses, usually *wuglet* or *wugling*, become much commoner among teenagers, though several suggested *miniwug* or *microwug*. This ties in with an explosion of *mini-* and *micro-* prefixes in the language as a whole. The *mini-/micro-* rocket took off in the 1960s, with words such as *minicar, minibar, miniskirt, and microwave* becoming commonplace. From then on, *mini-* cropped up everywhere: 'I must have been out of my *mini-mind*', commented one writer.

Confidence in handling word formation may be one reason behind a leap in vocabulary which occurs around the age of thirteen. It's a skill non-native speakers find hard to master. Sometimes words they think should exist, simply do not: 'A principle . . . of idealization . . . is applied *manywhere*', said a Japanese scientist in the preface to his book.

But every time we speak, we have to pick from this huge number of words, old and new. At one time, searching for a word was assumed to be like hunting for a book in a library. A person went to the shelf in the mental lexicon where it was stored, as it were, then pulled it out. If this selection took place in too much of a hurry, a neighbour might be accidentally picked, such as *left* instead of 'right', or *geranium* instead of 'hydrangea'.

But this neat library model is unlikely. It is more as if

humans pull out a number of words from the bookshelves all at once, and then replace those they do not want. The mind subconsciously overprepares itself, by activating more words than can be used. The most direct evidence comes from blends, when two or more words are combined into one, as in 'She *chuttled*' from *chuckled* and *chortled*, 'It's cold in *Greeceland*', a blend of *Greenland* and *Iceland*, but said in a Greek restaurant. 'He was given a *standing applause*', said a politician, blending a 'standing ovation' with 'loud applause'. Another time, the government were accused of *shrugging their feet* over an important issue: the speaker presumably meant either 'shrugging their shoulders' or 'dragging their feet'.

Both meaning and sound are interwoven in the selection process. A musician commented about the conductor Toscanini: 'He had very little *symphony* with modern music', meaning 'sympathy'. The words sound similar, and Toscanini often conducted symphonies. Both were probably aroused in the mind, then the wrong one selected (see figure 4.3). Such errors indicate that it is normal to prepare more words than are needed, and to suppress those which are unwanted. Sometimes the wrong word is suppressed.

An initial idea progressively fans out, it seems, and spreads to associated words. Eventually, numerous different words may be ready to go, all of them resembling the word required in some way or other. Words that fit both the sound and the meaning get progressively more aroused, and others fade away. Finally, a winner will pop up, like toast out of a toaster, occasionally the

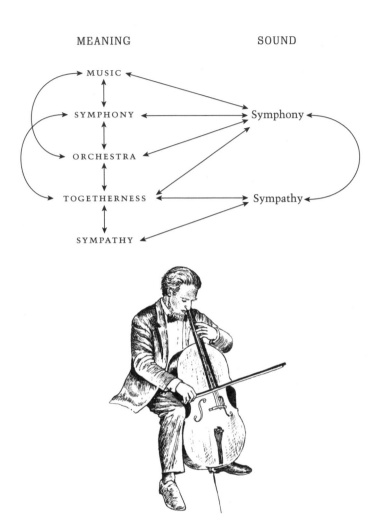

MEANING   SOUND

MUSIC

SYMPHONY   Symphony

ORCHESTRA

TOGETHERNESS   Sympathy

SYMPATHY

Slip of the tongue: he had very little symphony [sympathy] with modern music.

4.3 Over-preparation of words

wrong one, if there are two or more similar candidates. All of
this happens in less time than an eyeblink.

So many words are aroused, because so many words are
linked. The human word-web is not two-dimensional, or even
three-dimensional, it's multi-dimensional. In a Michael Frayn
play, *Alphabetical order*, a character tries to find where a secre-
tary filed an important piece of information: 'Most probably
she'll have it filed under whoever said it, which we don't know,
or the occasions he said it upon, which we don't know either.
But conceivably she may also . . . have it under . . . Corporal
Punishment. Or Punishment Corporal. Or Labour Party. Or
Parties Labour.' The human mind would probably have
filed it in all these places.

But manipulating the vast, intertwined web of words
inevitably leads to short cuts. Narrowing down the options
can involve unseen snares. These will be discussed in the next
chapter. Yet how lucky most of us are that we can so quickly
locate the words we need out of the 50,000 or so we have stored.
Our skill in doing this becomes apparent perhaps only when
compared to someone who has lost this ability, as sometimes
happens to stroke victims. This frustrating condition is
described in Nabokov's *Pale fire*:

> She still could speak. She paused and groped and found
> What seemed at first a serviceable sound,
> But from adjacent cells impostors took
> The place of words she needed, and her look
> Spelt imploration as she sought in vain
> To reason with the monsters in her brain.

The language web

Words are often felt to hold magical power. A survivor from the *Titanic* reportedly said: 'My maiden name was Trout: how could I possibly drown?' But the most magical aspect is probably the huge number of words we know, and the speed with which we find the ones we want.

❺ A world-wide web
Options and snares

By degrees I made a discovery of still greater moment. I found that these people possessed a method of communicating their experience and feelings to one another by articulate sounds. I perceived that the words they spoke sometimes produced pleasure or pain, smiles or sadness, in the minds and countenances of the hearers. This was indeed a godlike science, and I ardently desired to become acquainted with it.

Mary Shelley Frankenstein (1818)

We human beings are odd compared with our nearest animal relatives. We've lost most of our hair, we wear clothes, and according to the writer Mark Twain, we are the only animal who blushes, or who needs to. But our oddest characteristic is our language.

Unlike animals, we humans can say what we want, when we want. 'Alfred burned the cakes', 'Amanda plans to breed bandicoots' and 'Mermecolions intrigue me', are all possible utterances, even though Alfred burned the cakes over 1,000 years ago, Amanda's bandicoot-breeding plans are in the future, and mermecolions are mythical creatures, a cross between a lion and an ant with sex organs the wrong way round.

This open-endedness, the ability to talk about anything at any time is uniquely human. In contrast, many animals are limited in the signals they can send. One species of grasshopper selects between six possible chirps, meaning roughly: 'Life is good', 'Get off my patch!', 'I'm feeling sexy', 'That female's mine!', 'How about making love?' and finally, 'I did enjoy that!' It is as if humans had to choose between 'Hello', 'Goodbye' and 'I love you.'

Animals, then, are linguistically limited, but all normal humans can produce and understand any number of new words and sentences. Humans use the multiple options of language often without thinking. But blindly, they sometimes fall into its traps. They are like spiders who exploit their webs, but themselves get caught in the sticky strands. In this final chapter, I want to discuss how the huge choice available to us also sets up possible snares.

The human mind subconsciously cuts down on the potential language pathways, and in so doing ensnares the thoughts of its speakers. It is a tangle which humans either make for themselves, or is made for them by skilful persuaders.

Persuasion is of course a major use of language, maybe one of its original uses. Everyone needs to be on their guard. Overt mind-bending is usually easy to detect. Before elections, politicians are clearly trying to influence us, and advertisements go in for obvious mind-bashing: 'The great taste of grapefruit. Cool, refreshing, full of flavour. Wholesome, natural grapefruit – the colour of the sun.' But less direct persuasion may trap the unwary.

Language worries worth worrying about do exist. They rarely appear to be major perils, but like a banana skin, or a loose paving stone, they can trip people up, and cause more damage than might be foreseen. A single strand in a spider's web might at first catch a fly by one leg, but then entrap it further. Speakers therefore need to watch out. If they clear their minds of pseudo-worries, such as anxiety about split infinitives, then they might have more energy left to notice these genuine pitfalls.

The 'gobbledegook syndrome' is the most straightforward of these snares. Gobbledegook can be defined as pretentious or unintelligible jargon, as when a young man impresses others with 'idle chatter of a transcendental kind' in Gilbert and Sullivan's opera *Patience*. Gobbledegook needs to be 'translated' into comprehensible language – though it must not be confused with technical vocabulary. A doctor talking to another doctor might justifiably use words such as electroencephalography or mesenteric adenitis. However, medical terms can become gobbledegook if used inappropriately: 'Is there any history of cardiac arrest in your family?' a doctor asked. 'We never had no trouble with the police', was the indignant reply.

Politically correct terms are sometimes labelled gobbledegook. But this is not entirely justified. The PC movement has some beneficial spin-offs. *Firefighter* or *bar-person* in an ad makes it clear that either sex can apply. The PC movement is still young, and some PC phrases sound very bureaucratic, as with *visually challenged* for 'blind', or *developmentally inconvenienced* for the older term 'mentally retarded'. But PC hearts are in the right place, even if their tongues or pens are twisted up in sesquipedalian words.

PC phrases need to be looked at unemotionally one by one. Some terms merely reflect a normal distinction between written language, which is fairly formal, and spoken language, which is relatively informal. Other expressions overlap with euphemisms – though these rarely present a serious threat to understanding. It does not need a linguist to point out that the bus company which *restructured* its fares was just raising them. Or that *workforce imbalance correction* simply means sacking people, or that someone who is *disturbed* is mentally ill (see figure 5.1).

In sentence structure, gobbledegook is usually due to lack of time and care, as perhaps with the personal pension plan which defined 'foreign emoluments' as 'earnings of a person resident but not domiciled in the United Kingdom from duties performed wholly or partly in the United Kingdom for a non-resident employer'. It is as clear as dirty-dishwater, and perhaps more time should have been spent on drafting it. Clear, concise writing cannot be done in a hurry, as the French writer Pascal realized when he once wrote to a friend: 'I have made this letter longer than usual, only because I have not had time to make it shorter.'

The diversion of the MENTALLY DISORDERED from the criminal justice and penal systems needs to be seen against the background of the management of the MENTALLY DISORDERED in general.

Hospitals were equipped for the longer-term treatment of severely MENTALLY DISTURBED patients.

Witnesses testified to Mr R's DISTURBED BEHAVIOUR from the moment of his arrest.

Many of the nation's most DISTURBED have been transferred from institutions to southbound Victoria Line trains, with strict instructions not to get off until the end of the line.

In the early days of nursing people here, it was basically restraint of patients expressing BIZARRE BEHAVIOUR.

An owner whose pattern of behaviour … borders on the BIZARRE.

MAD

INSANE

MENTALLY DISORDERED

MENTALLY DISTURBED

DISTURBED (BEHAVIOUR)

BIZARRE (BEHAVIOUR)

5.1 Political correctness – euphemism overlap

So gobbledegook delays understanding, and can also cause misunderstanding. Only recently a Member of the European Parliament commented: 'The treaties are so complicated that very few people can possibly understand what they mean . . . Fraudsters are having a field day . . . simply because the regulations are so complex.'

Overall, gobbledegook is easy to spot, though less easy to cure, because lucid speaking and writing require time and practice. But it is worth making the effort. Good communicators are like cooks squeezing a lemon. They extract the essence, then convey the full flavour to the consumers, whether in speech or writing.

But another language trap, the 'wimp effect' is more subtle. Humans subconsciously notice which words occur together. Newspapers kept reminding us that George Bush had shaken off his *wimp* image: 'President Bush has decisively buried his lingering image as a White House wimp', we were told. But in so doing, they were reinforcing his negative image. The repeated *Bush–wimp* pairing ensured that he remains perhaps permanently associated with wimphood, however undeservedly.

And in a newspaper report about the New York police force, the word *corruption* occurred sixty-five times. An enquiry was only just starting, yet the consistent nearness of the words *police* and *corruption*, as in 'police corruption power and analysis unit', guaranteed that New Yorkers would feel anxious about their police even before any investigation had taken place.

So humans may be subconsciously trapped by their language. Linguistic freedom was seriously questioned over sixty years ago, first by Edward Sapir, then by Benjamin Lee Whorf, two American linguists. Their ideas became known as the Sapir–Whorf hypothesis. Sapir stated: 'Human beings do not live in the objective world alone . . . but are very much at the mercy of their particular language . . . The worlds in which different societies live are distinct worlds, not merely the same world with different labels attached.'

Their detailed claims are far from clear – though they undoubtedly cover much more than the common observation that some cultures have more subdivisions than others for particular vocabulary areas. By the way, the most-quoted example, that Eskimos have numerous words for *snow*, has been grossly exaggerated, as explained in an article aptly titled 'The great Eskimo vocabulary hoax'. British skiers possibly outdo Eskimos, or more accurately, speakers of the Inuit language, in the varieties of snow they can name.

Whorf's best known claim was that 'standard average European' cultures are in a mental straitjacket in which events are packaged into boxes, such as *days, hours, minutes*: a length of time, he argued, 'is envisioned as a row of similar units, like a row of bottles'. In the American-Indian language Hopi, a different linguistic situation prevails, he suggested. An English utterance such as 'They stayed ten days' becomes in Hopi: 'They stayed until the eleventh day' or 'They left after the tenth day.' In Hopi, according to Whorf, 'Our "length of time"' is not regarded as a length but as a 'relation between two events in lateness'.

But all Whorf has pointed out here is that the Hopi language expresses 'time' in a different way from English. Hopi and English speakers need not envisage time differently: it is a hypothesis which needs to be tested, and which he himself failed to test.

So Sapir and Whorf tried to identify possible language traps. They may have been struggling to express an even wider entrapment in language, which I call 'the frog-in-a-well' problem. This comes from a Chinese folk tale about a frog which had lived all its life in a well. One day it hopped out, and was astonished to find what a limited view of the world it had always had.

In English, a clear example of this is the use of generic *he*, that is, *he* supposedly referring to either sex. A widespread assumption exists that use of *he* for 'he *and* she' presents no problem, especially if a disclaimer is attached: 'When I say *he*, I mean "he" or "she".'

But *he* is far from neutral: both men and women assume generic *he* refers primarily to men. In a typical study, twenty university students, ten men and ten women, were asked to listen to a number of sentences, such as: 'When a botanist is in the field, he is usually working', and say in each case, as quickly as possible, 'Yes' if the sentence could refer to a female, or 'No' if the sentence could not refer to a female. Ninety-five per cent of the subjects, both males and females, made errors, and said that *he*-sentences could not refer to females. But when the sentence was changed to a genuinely sex-neutral wording, such as: 'A botanist who is in the field is usually working', the number who assumed that the sentence did not include females dropped to forty-three per cent.

86

A world-wide web

In another study, ten university students, five men and five women, were asked to read paragraphs involving a neutral-between-sexes person, such as 'beginning writer', but which contained the pronoun *he*. Afterwards, they were asked if the 'beginning writer' was male, female, or unspecified. Only twenty per cent consistently said 'unspecified'. And there are numerous similar studies.

Humans behave like spiderlings who never venture outside their web. They create their own limited mental pictures of the world. The word *week* is often quoted. A week has no concrete reality in the external world. Yet most native speakers of English have a mental model of a sequence of seven days, which is divided into two chunks, five working days followed by two rest-days, the 'weekend' – or sometimes it's six working days followed by one rest day. They have this idealized notion of a week, even though they may organize their *own* working life quite differently, and may know that technically the week begins on a Sunday. In contrast, an Inca week had nine days, eight working days followed by market day, on which the king changed wives (see figure 5.2).

These mental models can be handed down from generation to generation, and they can reinforce cultural norms. The word *mother* represents a cluster of at least three different ideas, as the linguist George Lakoff has pointed out: first, a birth idea, the mother gives birth to the child; second, a nurturing idea, the mother looks after the child; third, a marital idea, the mother is the wife of the father. This cluster of ideas has helped to give rise to a stereotype of a 'proper mother' as one who gives birth,

ENGLISH

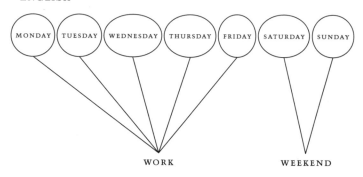

INCA

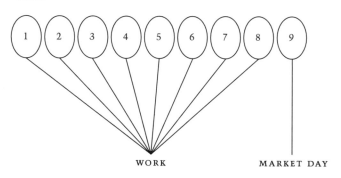

5.2 English and Inca weeks

stays at home and nurtures, and is married to the father. The stereotype persists, even though it is increasingly out of touch with modern society.

To take another example, many British people assume that they live in a society organized in tiers. They have a mental model of a layer-cake, with rich upper-class at the top, comfortably off middle-class in the centre, and struggling working-class at the bottom. Yet numerous socio-economic studies have shown that the middle-class versus working-class divide is one of differing life-styles, not position on an economic hierarchy. As an actor noted: 'We were poor, but we had a piano, so I suppose we were middle-class.'

Powerful mental images may be preserved or even created by metaphors, it has been suggested. Expressions such as 'Pauline was *rich* in ideas', 'Alan had a *wealth* of experience' presuppose that accumulating money might be a praiseworthy aim.

Consider the emotion of anger. This is often envisaged as heated liquid in a container, as George Lakoff has pointed out. It is like a whistling kettle which builds up a head of steam: 'Mark's anger simmered', 'Helen seethed with rage', 'Neil's blood boiled.' Overheated liquid is liable to burst out, as in 'Mary blew her top', 'Matthew exploded.'

Such metaphors reflect genuine mental images, according to psycholinguistic experiments. When asked about an idiom such as 'hit the roof', speakers envisaged containers bursting open and their contents spouting upwards. They did not imagine a person with springs on their heels hitting their head on the ceiling.

Arguably, the 'liquid in a container' image could lead people to assume that explosion is a natural consequence of overheating, and justify outbursts of rage. This is unlike the situation in some parts of India, where anger is still thought of as heat, but dry heat which requires lubrication. So universal tendencies may have different cultural manifestations.

Fear provides the reverse scenario. Physiologically, humans either freeze or flee. Yet almost all English metaphors stress freezing or empty containers, not fleeing: 'Peter froze with terror', 'Marigold was rooted to the spot', 'Peggy's limbs turned icy cold', 'Paul's courage drained away.' A petrified English speaker might stand still, rather than attempt to escape. It is a worrying possibility, though one which has not yet been checked out.

But entrapment in existing, traditional metaphors, is not the only danger. Metaphor is a powerful device for changing people's attitudes. 'Nukespeak' is the most publicized example. Phrases such as 'nuclear shields', 'nuclear umbrella', might lead people to assume that nuclear devices are essential safety equipment, it has been argued, and distract attention from their potential danger. The 'surgical' language of the Gulf War described air-strikes as having 'pin-point accuracy', in the hope of persuading people that the war damaged only buildings rather than humans, it has been claimed.

Metaphors are 'high tech' devices for changing people's minds. The linguist Susan Elgin used to get annoyed when friends she was visiting left their television on. She found it insulting. Then she read that for the younger generation, 'the television is the flickering fire on the hearth'. The metaphor changed everything for her – instantly. She now understood why the television set was left on, and was no longer annoyed by it. She comments: 'I wouldn't expect them to put out the fire in their fireplace during my visit: why should they turn off their television?'

Metaphors used by politicians and journalists can affect attitudes: humans can be dehumanized by aligning them with illness, as when Ronald Reagan vowed to fight the 'communist cancer', or with animals, as when couriers who carry drugs are referred to as ants or mules. An electronics firm which was faring badly was said to have 'binged on the 1980s consumer boom' and was now 'attempting to recover from the hangover'. The metaphor of bingeing implies some degree of foolhardiness rather than sheer economic bad luck.

But metaphors do not automatically catch on and influence people: they have to fit in with a feeling in the air, or Zeitgeist, which differs from language to language. In psycho-babble, metaphors have to achieve cultural resonance, and avoid cognitive dissonance, since we humans are like spiders who get accustomed to moving along some strands of our web, and not others.

A few images are widely accepted. A notion that 'up' is good, and 'down' is bad may be universal. 'Paula's going up in the world', 'Jack's down on his luck', 'Henrietta's moving up the ladder.' These may have equivalents everywhere. But other images are local. It is not chance that when dealing with large quantities of, say, drugs, Europeans across the channel tend to talk about avalanches, but we in Britain refer to floods.

Or consider wine. Wine drinkers are prepared to believe that wine can be breezy, flabby, tough, chunky, chocolatey, meaty or even chewy (see figure 5.3) – but puzzlement and fury erupted when a wine critic suggested a wine smelt of hamster cages, and worse. As a wine editor acidly commented: 'Things like "cobwebs", "sumo wrestler's jockstraps" and "unswept floorboards" simply don't belong in a tasting note.'

Successful metaphors have to be both sufficiently ear-catching to make people take notice, but sufficiently ordinary to be acceptable. An organization might be called an octopus: most people know an octopus has eight legs which reach out and cling and pull. But to call it a starfish or a squid would be unlikely to have the same effect, because people are less aware of how these animals behave. So the moral is twofold. Watch out for clever metaphors which might bend your mind. And conversely, if you yourself want to influence anyone, use metaphor, though use it carefully.

But what about language itself? Metaphor has shaped, perhaps misshaped, our views about how it works. The most widely used metaphor is that of a game. The image is an oldish one. At the beginning of this century, the Swiss linguist de Saussure suggested that language was like a game of chess, in which all the pieces are interdependent. Just as a single chess piece such as a knight acquires a value only in relation to the other chess pieces on the board, the same is true of pieces of language. And the philosopher Wittgenstein also talked about language as a game.

It is tough and chunky, pummelling your mouth with tannin and sheer force of personality.

Chocolate and strawberries with a lean dry streak of earthy reserve.

Wine of marvellous minty, blackcurranty perfume, with some of the cedar and cigar smoke spice of the great Medocs, and a caressing gentleness of texture.

The fumes of new oak spice linger over the glass even in the wine's most stubborn adolescent sulks.

The piercing acid/sweetness of blackcurrant juice pressed straight from the bush, sweetened and perfumed with a few drops of juice from ripe raspberries and an earthiness like fields after summer rain.

Liquorice and peach fruit, freshened up with mountain herbs and the snappy acidity of lime.

5.3 Acceptable wine imagery

The game image is useful. But all metaphors can potentially mislead, in that any metaphor fits only partially. The game metaphor fits the rule-governed nature of language. But it perhaps over-emphasizes its neatness and tidiness.

A more revealing image, now that we know more about language, may be the *language web*, the image and title of this book. The language web is potentially vast, though each language exploits only a small part of the available possibilities. We might laugh at daleks and other fictional robots with their narrow range of vocabulary and speech sounds. But we humans are similarly limited in our thoughts.

As speakers we behave in our use of language like surfers on the World Wide Web. Those who browse in this extensive computer network soon find time runs out, just as it would if a spider were to try and cover the whole network of its own web. In the circumstances, we narrow down the number of tracks we go along, and select a few recurring routes. Ultimately, we must take care not to behave like the Chinese frog, which jumped back into its well because it could not stand the freedom outside.

This World Wide Web notion ties in with current ideas about how the mind works. Up till a few years ago, standard digital computers provided the major metaphor for human language processes, yet this analogy has not proved particularly fruitful. Old-style computers worked in too rigid a way. Now the brain itself is being taken as a source of inspiration for understanding the mind, and also, incidentally, for devising new computers: 'We wish to replace the "computer metaphor" of the mind with the "brain metaphor" as a model of the mind', said two leading cognitive scientists. Increasingly, the brain is turning out to be like a massive spider's web with its numerous circuits and multiple interconnections. We ourselves narrow these down in a way that is inevitable, yet merits serious thought.

But to recap: this book began with a cobweb of worries which I attempted to clear away. We need to understand language, I argued, not try to control it. Then I tried to extend understanding of language: how it began, how children acquire it, and how humans remember the huge web of words. Out of this wider framework, some genuine concerns emerged.

Yet there is one extra worry to add in, language loss. Ninety per cent of the world's languages may be in danger. Around 6,000 languages are currently spoken in the world. Of these, half are moribund in that they are no longer learned by the new generation of speakers. A further 2,500 are in a danger zone, in that they have fewer than a hundred thousand speakers. This leaves around 600, a mere ten per cent of the current total, as likely survivors a century from now. Of course, languages inevitably split, just as Latin eventually split into the various Romance languages. So some new languages may emerge. But the diversity will be much reduced. The splendiferous bouquet of current languages will be whittled down to a small posy with only a few different flowers.

'Worry about words . . . ', the writer A. P. Herbert once said. 'For whatever else you may do, you will be using words always.

All day, and every day, words matter. Before you die the aeroplane may be as out of date as the rickshaw . . . But words will still matter.' He was quite right to tell us to worry about words. But, I would like to add, it is important to worry about them in the right way.

Afterword

Stirring up a hornets' nest: responses
to the Reith lectures

'Madam, HOW DARE YOU distort, desecrate and defile the
English language as you did in your recent Reith lecture . . .', ran
a letter in my postbag. It was one of many responses to my Reith
lectures, some angry, others supportive: 'I am delighted that you
were chosen to give the Reith lectures . . . those of us who love
the language need a champion and now know that we have one!'

Some letters were bafflingly hostile: 'Well missy, and what
are you going to be when you grow up?' But others were truly
heart-warming: 'Forgive me – a total stranger (unless we met at
either L's eightieth or ninetieth birthday parties) taking up your
valuable time. It is mainly to thank you for the pleasure you
have given two old people with your first Reith lecture.'

Journalists too were divided. 'Jean Aitchison has hit on pre-
ciscly the right combination of novelty and controversy', said
Robert Hanks in *The Independent*. 'Mind your language, professor' was the *Evening Standard* headline, where A. N. Wilson
announced that 'What the professor says is half-baked, half
true, and misses the essential point.'

Perhaps I should have been prepared. 'What Aitchison has
embarked upon, she may not realize, is the linguistic equiva-

Jean Aitchison
documents the
furious reaction to
her Reith lectures on
language

"Madam, how dare you distort, desecrate and defile the English language..."

"Madam, How dare you distort, desecrate and defile the English language as you did in your recent Reith lecture . . ." ran a letter in my postbag — one of many responses to my recent BBC Reith lectures on Radio 4. Some of the letters and comments I received were angry, others supportive: "Jean Aitchison has hit on precisely the right combination of novelty and controversy," said Robert Hanks in *The Independent*.

The Reith lectures were inaugurated in 1948 in honour of Lord Reith, director general of the BBC from 1927 to 1938. The topics range. The first set was given by Bertrand Russell, and last year's by the architect Sir Richard Rogers. This year, it was the turn of language.

With my first lecture, I unwittingly banged the linguistic funny bone of Radio 4 regulars. The response amazed me. My pleasure at those who enjoyed the lectures was mixed with astonishment at those who ranted at me. All quite puzzling to someone who works at Oxford, where lecturers receive mainly "goal-directed attention". Students are attentive if they perceive a lecture to be directly usable in examinations, and are, at most, politely interested if not.

Perhaps I should have been prepared: "What Aitchison has embarked upon, she may not realise, is the linguistic equivalent of launching an anti-war speech in the Pentagon," said Mark Lawson in *The Guardian*. For Hanks, my lecture was "all perfectly sensible advice, but handing it out to Radio 4 audiences is like trying to set the Shipping Forecast to theology". "Professor Jean Aitchison should bring a few million pedants swinging out of their trees," said Harold Jackson in *The Guardian*. And so it transpired.

"A woman who hates English as it is writ" flamed the headline in the *Daily Mail* over an article in which Paul Johnson alleged that my ideas were "a frontal assault on the rules of the English language". "Mind your language, professor" was the *Evening Standard* headline, where A. N. Wilson announced that "What the professor says is half-baked, half true, and misses the essential point".

The angry buzz was "all summarised by Philip Howard in *The Times*: "The Reith lecturer has poked her stick into a hornets' nest. Out buzz the crusties swollen with venom, stinging Jean Aitchison for permissiveness about language . . ." Howard used to write an informative column on words himself, and he sprang to my defence: "Who are these prescriptivists . . . ? they are white, middle-class, middle-browed males, middle-aged temperamentally if not temporally . . . They . . . find themselves in a new world, surrounded by new ideas, new words, new grammar . . . Their problem is not the decay of English, but the male menopause".

My lecture plan for the series was straightforward. "The language web" was the title, because webs can both enable and ensnare, and also because

they have a preordained overall pattern. First, I discussed the cobweb of false worries that surrounds language. I then suggested how language evolved in the human species, how children acquire it, and how educated English speakers remember 50,000 or more words. Finally, I stressed that people are right to be concerned about language, though not in the ways traditionally assumed. But sweeping away the cobwebs was wishful thinking. The buzzing hornets fell into several categories.

"One-word worriers" were the most straightforward, people perturbed by my presumed misuse of a particular word, such as my pronunciation of kilQmetre: "I was saddened to hear you use that unattractive Americanism KilQmetre . . . why not (correctly) kIlometre?"

"I was astonished . . . to hear you pronounce kilometre as kilOmeter. Surely, even if it is argued that language has no rights or wrongs, but merely usage, there IS sense and nonsense. The pronunciation kilOmeter is in the latter category, kIlometre in the former." Current usage suggests that both pronunciations are common. John Wells, professor of phonetics at London University reported views on some disputed usages in his authoritative *Longman Pronunciation Dictionary*. He notes that 52 per cent preferred the traditional kIlometre, and 48 per

6 I was saddened to hear you use that unattractive Americanisation KilQmetre... why not (correctly) KIlometre 9

cent the newer kilOmetre. Clearly, two opposing influences are at work: measurements such as centimetre, millimetre, have stress on the first syllable, favouring kIlometre, but words ending in -ometer as thermometer, barometer, have stress on the second syllable, favouring kilOmetre, the pronunciation which is found in American English. Yet competing alternatives are a sign that a change may be underway. Old established forms are not automatically "right", and the language often selects for itself the variant which fits in best with current language patterns.

A second set of complaints came from the "cloth ears brigade", those who had simply not heard what I said. "The speech patterns you endorse are the direct result of downright bone idleness in the speech of the cockneys," claimed one letter writer — even though the most noticeable cockney speech feature, the glottal stop, requires considerable muscular tension, and could not be due to laziness, as I had pointed out. "Professor Aitchison . . . misses the point that we only master language by learning its shapes, patterns, and yes, rules", huffed A. N. Wilson of the *Evening Standard*. Yet he himself has missed the point I made by failing to comprehend the distinction between genuine rules, those used subconsciously, and artificially imposed

prescriptions, such as a pedantic ban on split infinitives.

A third group of disapprovers were "gap leapers", those who leapt from a dislike of something I had said to a wider disapproval of my presumed life-style. "I find it a matter of deep regret that a person of your standing should support dirty talk on the media," ranted one letter-writer — apparently fired up by my statement that swearing is on the increase. The letter continued: "If you habitually hobnob with hippies, lesbians, drug users, Communists, etc, you may become used to it . . . I suggest you change your friends and keep better company." Yet I do not know any hippies, and have no idea whether my friends come into the other categories listed — though I would be surprised if they were drug-users, they are far too clear-headed. My mind is always boggling, according to Paul Johnson in the *Daily Mail*, and yes, he does make my mind boggle. It maxi-boggles when he claims that my linguistic views hand over a leftwing political message. My professional views about language have nothing to do with politics.

The "collapse of civilization" group is the most pessimistic. They adopt the "For want of a nail" scenario, where a lost nail led to a lost kingdom. Lack of care is presumed to lead to language collapse: "Clawing our way painfully and slowly from Neanderthal grunting, to Chaucer, Shakespeare, Dickens and Lord Reith, we shall descend swiftly to Neanderthal grunting again. What a waste!" someone lamented, even though I had stressed that language neatened its own patterns, and kept itself in check.

My first reaction to the furore was delight that so many people responded with interest to talks about language. My second reaction was puzzlement. Why did my lectures arouse such strong feelings? Why were so many listeners unwilling to believe what I said? After all, I have lectured on linguistics for more than a quarter of a century, and written several books on the topic — so I must know more about it than many people.

My lectures, it appears, challenged some deeply entrenched ideas about language — and such views are difficult to alter, whatever the evidence. Attitude change has long been a major interest of social psychologists. A source of authority can be persuasive, they note, but less so if the message contradicts strong beliefs. "It is not sufficient to lead the horse to the water; one must also push his head under water to get him to drink," a psychologist noted in the 1960s. But in the 1990s, it has become clear that even immersion does not necessarily force the horse to drink: it might simply kick till you let it go. This seems to be true of information about language.

I wonder if views will have changed by the time language comes round again as a Reith lecture topic? When it does, one of my correspondents from abroad is eager to deliver them: "The British intelligentsia can rest assured that the quality and standard of my lectures and their mode of delivery would be better than any Englishman's," his letter claimed. He hoped the BBC would "relish the noble idea of allowing me to teach English to the English . . . where a rot has palpably set in".

But as a final note, I waited impatiently for reactions to my second lecture, on the origin of language, the topic of my new book. The first letter firmly disillusioned me: "May I suggest that the simplest explanation of the origin of language is the biblical one — that God made men in His own image and likeness? As He is . . . a God who communicates, so He has made the human race able to communicate in verbal language." Well, where do I go from here?

Jean Aitchison is Rupert Murdoch professor of language and communication at Oxford University. Her book, The seeds of speech: Language origin and evolution *is published in April and the Reith lectures later this year, both by Cambridge University Press.*

From *The Times Higher Education Supplement*, 15 March 1996. © Times Supplements Ltd.

lent of delivering an anti-war speech in the Pentagon', said
Mark Lawson in *The Guardian*. For Robert Hanks in *The
Independent*, my first lecture was 'all perfectly sensible advice,
but handing it out to Radio 4 audiences is like trying to set the
Inquisition right on theology'. 'Professor Jean Aitchison should
bring a few million pedants swinging out of their trees', said
Harold Jackson in his preview column in *The Guardian*. And
so it transpired.

The head-butting of an aggressive stag trying to shelter its
mate and deerlet seems weak compared with the ferocity with
which some commentators defended deep-grooved ideas. 'A
woman wot hates English as it is writ' flamed the headline in
the *Daily Mail* above an article by Paul Johnson. 'In recent years
... BBC satraps have taken pleasure in having the Reith
Lectures delivered by eccentric academics, weirdos and female
harpies ...' he claimed. 'Jean Aitchison ... fits beautifully into
this pattern. Her ideas are a frontal assault on the rules of the
English language.' What is going on, he alleged is 'the usual
childishness we have come to expect from the clever, but funda-
mentally silly, people in charge of the BBC'. He particularly
reproached the BBC head of radio, Liz Forgan, whom he
denounced as 'an upper-middle-class revolutionary' who had
gone in for 'a career of mischief-making'. Liz Forgan responded
like a boxer matching punch for punch in the *Daily Mail* a few
days later.

'Up with this I will not put', was the headline above her
reply. 'There should be a penalty for the Improper Use of Paul
Johnson', she alleged. 'Off he goes with the same very loud

howling noise whenever a red handle is pulled, whether the approaching peril is women, the BBC, trendy academics, bad manners or atheism . . . This year's BBC Reith Lectures . . . given by the scholarly, eloquent and tough minded Oxford Professor Jean Aitchison, were guaranteed trouble. [She] . . . clearly merited the Magic Hazard Warning and sure enough "A woman wot hates English as it is writ" wailed out across the land . . . Powerful stuff radio!'

Forgan expressed delight that the Reith lectures should have started an argument in the popular press about language, but pointed out the naivety of lumping all intellectual women together. Unlike me, she dislikes split infinitives, for example. 'Keep breaking the glass, you make a lovely fire alarm', she exhorted Paul Johnson. But, she reminded him, 'Pay attention at the end of the first lecture to the words of the great Samuel Johnson . . .: " . . . to enchain syllables, and to lash the wind, are equally the undertakings of pride".'

Judging from newspaper comments, more males than females became alarmed by the lectures, as pointed out by Philip Howard in *The Times*, who summarized the angry buzz well: 'The Reith lecturer has poked her stick into a hornets' nest. Out buzz the crusties swollen with venom, stinging Jean Aitchison for permissiveness about language . . . ' Philip Howard used to write an informative column on words himself, and he sprang to my defence: 'Who are these prescriptivists . . . they are white, middle-class, middle-browed males, middle-aged temperamentally if not temporally . . . They . . . find themselves in a new world, surrounded by new ideas, new words, new grammar . . . Their problem is not the decay of English, but the male menopause.'

The buzzing hornets fell into several categories. 'One-word worriers' were the most straightforward, people perturbed by my presumed misuse of a particular word, such as my pronunciation of *kilOmetre*:

> 'I was saddened to hear you use that unattractive Americanism *kilOmetre* . . . why not (correctly) *kIlometre*?'
>
> 'I was astonished . . . to hear you pronounce *kilometre* as *kilOmeter* . . . Surely, even if it is argued that language has no rights or wrongs, but merely usage, there IS sense and nonsense. The pronunciation *kilOmeter* is in the latter category, *kIlometre* in the former.'

Current usage suggests that both pronunciations are common. John Wells, Professor of Phonetics at London University, reported views on some disputed usages in his authoritative *Longman pronunciation dictionary* (1990). He noted that fifty-two per cent preferred the traditional *kIlometre*, and forty-eight per cent the newer *kilOmetre*. Clearly, two opposing influences are at work: measurements such as *centimetre, millimetre*, have stress on the first syllable, favouring *kIlometre*, but words ending in *-ometer* as *thermometer, barometer*, have stress on the second syllable, favouring *kilOmetre*, the pronunciation which is found in American English. Yet competing alternatives are a sign that a change may be underway, as I said in the first lecture. Old established forms are not automatically 'right', and the language often selects for itself the variant which fits in best with current language patterns.

A second set of complaints came from the 'cloth ears brigade', those who had simply not heard what I said. 'The speech patterns you endorse are the direct result of downright bone-idleness in the speech of the cockneys', claimed one letter writer – even though the most noticeable cockney speech feature, the glottal stop, requires considerable muscular tension, and could not be due to laziness, as I had pointed out. 'Professor Aitchison . . . misses the point that we only master language by learning its shapes, patterns, and yes, rules', huffed A. N. Wilson of the *Evening Standard*. Yet he himself has missed the point I made by failing to comprehend the distinction between genuine rules, those used subconsciously, and artificially imposed prescriptions, such as a pedantic ban on split infinitives.

A third group of disapprovers were 'gap leapers', those who leapt from a dislike of something I had said to a wider disapproval of my presumed life-style. 'I find it a matter of deep regret that a person of your standing should support dirty talk on the media', ranted one letter-writer – apparently fired up by my statement that swearing is on the increase. The letter continued: 'If you habitually hobnob with hippies, lesbians, drug users, Communists, etc., you may become used to it . . . I suggest you change your friends and keep better company.' Yet I do not know any hippies, and have no idea whether my friends come into the other categories listed – though I would be surprised if they were drug-users, they are far too clear-headed. My mind is always boggling, according to Paul Johnson in the *Daily Mail*, and yes, he does make my mind boggle, it maxi-boggled when he claimed that my linguistic views were handing over a left-wing political message. My professional views about language have nothing to do with politics.

The 'collapse of civilization' crew were the most pessimistic. They adopted the 'for want of a nail' scenario, where a lost nail led to a lost battle. Lack of care is presumed to lead to language collapse: 'Clawing our way painfully and slowly from Neanderthal grunting, to Chaucer, Shakespeare, Dickens and Lord Reith, we shall descend swiftly to Neanderthal grunting again. What a waste!' lamented one correspondent – even though I had pointed out that language neatened its own patterns, and kept itself in check.

My first reaction to the furore was delight that so many people responded with interest to talks about language. My second reaction was puzzlement. Why did my lectures arouse such strong feelings? Why were so many listeners unwilling to believe what I said? After all, I have lectured on linguistics for more than a quarter of a century, and written several books on the topic – so I must know more about it than many people.

My lectures, it appears, challenged some deeply entrenched ideas about language – and such views are difficult to alter, whatever the evidence. Attitude change has long been a major interest of social psychologists. A source of authority can be persuasive, they note, but less so if the message contradicts strong beliefs. 'It is not sufficient to lead the horse to the water; one must also push his head under water to get him to drink', a psychologist noted in the 1960s. But in the 1990s, it has become clear that even immersion does not necessarily force the horse to drink: it might simply kick till you let it go. This seems to be true of information about language.

The first lecture caused the most fury. The BBC producer (Tessa Watt) had recommended that I should begin by meeting the prejudices of listeners head-on. I respected her judgement, but suggested that this was just a preliminary exercise 'Clearing the cobwebs', before moving on to truly interesting information about language. I waited with impatience for reactions to my second lecture, on the origin of language, the topic of my recent book, *The seeds of speech*. The first letter firmly disillusioned me: 'May I suggest that the simplest explanation of the origin of language is the biblical one – that God made men in His own image and likeness? As He is . . . a God who communicates, so He has made the human race able to communicate in verbal language.'

As they proceeded, the lectures evoked less agitation, and more support. At the end, Sue Gaisford in the *Independent on Sunday* summed it all up: 'Lord Reith can stop turning in his grave, smooth-down his legendary dinner-jacket and rest in peace for another year. The Reith Lectures are over and they weren't so bad after all. Fears that the Rupert Murdoch Professor would storm the mighty citadel of proper English dissolved into nothing . . . By the end she showed herself to be a cheerful, inventive custodian of our gloriously versatile language.'

But I wonder if views will have changed by the time language comes round again as a Reith lecture topic? When it does, one of my correspondents from abroad is eager to deliver them:

'The British intelligentsia can rest assured that the quality and standard of my lectures and their mode of delivery would be better than any Englishman's', his letter claimed. He hoped the BBC would 'relish the noble idea of allowing me to teach English to the English . . . where a rot has palpably set in'.

These comments on the responses to the Reith lectures are an expanded version of an article which appeared in *The Times Higher Education Supplement* 15 March 1996.

Notes

The notes below provide suggestions for further reading, further information about people and work mentioned in the text, and also sources for quotations. An alphabetical list of all linguistic works referred to is found under REFERENCES. Where two dates are given, the first is the date of the original publication, the second the date of a more accessible reprint.

Preface

QUOTATIONS: The quotation about the chattering toad is from Jacqueline Wilson, *Glubbslyme* (Oxford: Oxford University Press, 1987), p. 15. The Sherlock Holmes quotation is from A. Conan Doyle, 'A scandal in Bohemia', in *The adventures of Sherlock Holmes*, in *The complete Sherlock Holmes* (London: Penguin, 1894/1981), p. 162.

1   A web of worries

LANGUAGE CHANGE: Language change is dealt with in J. Aitchison, *Language change: Progress or decay?* 2nd edition (Cambridge: Cambridge University Press, 1991), which expands on a number of points made in this chapter. For a more extensive treatment of language change aimed primarily at university students, see A. McMahon, *Understanding language change* (Cambridge: Cambridge University Press, 1994).

QUOTATION: The quotation about rules at the beginning of the chapter is from G. Wagner, *On the wisdom of words* (London: George Allen and Unwin, 1968), p. 199.

COMPLAINTS: The complaints in the first paragraph are from Reuben Glass, *The Guardian*, 13 July 1982; Godfrey Talbot, president of the Queen's English

Society, quoted in 'Grapevine', *Sunday Times*, 16 June 1991; Gordon Connelly, in a letter to the *Sunday Times*, 21 March 1993.

WHALE SONGS: Changing whale songs are discussed in R. Payne, 'Humpbacks: their mysterious songs', in *National Geographic* 155 (1 January 1979), pp. 18–25.

CHAUCER ON LANGUAGE CHANGE: 'In forme of speche is chaunge': Geoffrey Chaucer's comment is from *Troylus and Criseyde* II, 1.22, and the longer passage surrounding it is quoted in fig. 1.1 (p. 3).

SAUSSURE'S VIEW ON 'ABSURD IDEAS': Ferdinand de Saussure's comment on the absurd ideas which surround language is in F. de Saussure, *Cours de linguistique générale* (Paris: Payot, 1915), p. 22. The translation of the sentence quoted is my own. For an English translation of the whole book, see F. de Saussure, *Course in general linguistics*, translated by W. Baskin (New York: The Philosophical Library, 1959; London: Fontana, 1974). Saussure is sometimes referred to as a 'father' of modern linguistics.

GRATING TOOTH-GNASHING: The fourteenth-century monk who complained about English was Ranulph Higden, of Chester, who died in 1364. His comments were translated by John Trevisa 1387, and are quoted in B. Cottle, *The triumph of English* (London: Blandford Press, 1969), p. 19.

SAMUEL JOHNSON ON 'DEGENERATION': Samuel Johnson's remark that tongues have 'a natural tendency to degeneration' occurs in the preface to his *Dictionary of the English language* (1755). A facsimile edition has been published by the Longman Group Ltd (1990). A CD-ROM version has been produced by Cambridge University Press (1996), which contains both the first (1755) edition and the fourth (1773) edition.

JONATHAN SWIFT ON REGULATING USAGE: Jonathan Swift's letter to the Lord Treasurer (1712) urging the formation of an academy to regulate language usage is published as 'Proposal for correcting, improving and ascertaining the English tongue', and is printed in J. Swift, *The prose works*, edited by H. Davis and L. Landa, vol. 4 (Oxford: Blackwell, 1957).

LANGUAGE RULES: Noah Webster's comment on the influence of Greek and Latin is in *Dissertations on the English language* (1789). Linguists draw a distinction between *prescriptive* rules, those which are artificially imposed, and *descriptive* rules, those which describe linguistic behaviour. For discussions of language prescriptivism, see R. W. Bailey, *Images of English* (Cambridge: Cambridge University Press, 1992); D. Cameron, *Verbal hygiene* (London: Routledge, 1995); T. Crowley, *The politics of discourse:*

The standard language question in British cultural debates (London: Macmillan, 1989), published in USA under the title: *Standard English and the politics of language* (Urbana: University of Illinois); J. Milroy and L. Milroy, *Authority in language: Investigating language prescription and standardization*, 2nd edition (London: Routledge, 1991); L. Mugglestone, *'Talking proper': The rise of accent as social symbol* (Oxford: Oxford University Press, 1995).

DOUBLE NEGATIVES: Chaucer's lines about the courteous knight occur in the *Prologue* to the *Canterbury Tales*, 1.70–3. Robert Lowth's prohibitions on the double negative occur in R. Lowth, *A short introduction to English grammar* (Menston, England: The Scholar Press, 1762/1967, facsimile reprint). John Earle's statement that the double negative is 'contrary to reason' is quoted in Crowley, *The politics of discourse*, p. 150. The details of how double negatives faded out from standard English are still unclear, as is the exact timing.

DIFFERENT FROM: The letter-writer who was irritated by *different to* is D. Partner, *Evening News* (December 1968). Thomas Dekker's use in the seventeenth century of *different to* is quoted in the *Oxford English Dictionary*, which contains several further early examples of *different to*. Fowler's comment that a preference for *different from* is a 'superstition' is in H. W. Fowler, *Modern English usage* (Oxford: Oxford University Press, 1926). Unhappiness about *different to* or *different than* was listed as one of the 'top ten' complaints made by BBC listeners by David Crystal, 'Language on the air – has it degenerated?', *The Listener*, 9 July 1981. Opinions vary as to how the preference originated: it may have been an attempt to make the word *different* behave in a parallel way to the verb *differ*. A suggestion that Latin was the cause is hard to substantiate.

ALICE'S COMPLAINT: Alice's complaint to the king is in Lewis Carroll's *Alice in Wonderland*, ch. 12, p. 113.

ETIQUETTE BOOKS, SPEECH AND MORALS: 'Censor' is named as the author of *Don't. A manual of mistakes and improprieties more or less prevalent in conduct and speech*, 1st edition, around 1880; 2nd edition (Whitstable: Pryor Press, 1982). The examples of *anyone . . . they* in figure 1.2 are from a leaflet produced under the auspices of the Australian Attorney-General's Department as part of the Corporations Law Simplification Program, extracts from which were printed in *Clarity* 34 (1966), pp. 29–33. *Clarity* is a movement to simplify legal language. The passage from *Groombridge's*

Annual Reader (1867) is quoted in Mugglestone '*Talking proper*', p. 310.
The statement by Norman Tebbit, November 1985, is quoted by D. Graddol
and J. Swann, 'Trapping linguists', in *Language and communication* 2
(1982), pp. 95–111.

DAMP TEASPOON SYNDROME: Certain language usages were likened to the
use of a damp spoon in the sugar bowl by Mary Stott, *The Guardian*, 9
September 1968. Max Müller's notions on laziness are in F. Max Müller,
Lectures on the science of language, vol. 2 (London: Routledge and
Thoemmes Press, 1994; first published in 1861 by London: Longman
Green). The drunken speech experiment was carried out by L. Lester and R.
Skousen, 'The phonology of drunkenness', in *Papers from the Parasession
on Natural Phonology* (Chicago: Chicago Linguistics Society, 1974). The
omission of past tense endings in spoken speech is described in A. C.
Gimson and A. Cruttenden, *Gimson's pronunciation of English*, 5th
edition, revised by A. Cruttenden (London: Arnold, 1994), which notes
(p. 261) that 'Such elision appears to take place most readily when /t/ or /
d/ is the middle one of three consonants.'

CRUMBLING CASTLE VIEW: This view is put forward by J. Simon, *Paradigms lost*
(London: Chatto and Windus, 1981), p. 211. The blue-footed booby is discussed in S. J. Gould, *Hens' teeth and horses' toes* (London: Penguin, 1983/
1984). The word *autochrondria* is documented in J. Ayto, *The Longman register of new words*, vol. 1 (London: Longman, 1989). Donna Karan used the
form *beared* in a television interview. *Shooted up* occurred in *The
Guardian*, 9 February 1990. *Blanded out* occurred in the *New Musical
Express*, 4 June 1988, quoted in J. Ayto, *The Longman register of new words*,
vol. 2 (London: Longman, 1990). The complaint about *a graffiti* was made by
D. M. Annett in a letter to the *Daily Telegraph*, 25 October 1980.

INFECTIOUS DISEASE ASSUMPTION: This was put forward by Douglas Bush,
'Polluting our language', in *American scholar* (Spring 1972), pp. 238–47.
The quotation about 'floating germs' occurs on p. 242. *Jocks* and *Burnouts*
are discussed in P. Eckert, 'Adolescent social structure and the spread of
linguistic change', in *Language in Society* 17 (1988), pp. 183–207, and in
P. Eckert, *Jocks and Burnouts: Social categories and identity in the high
school* (New York: Teachers College Press, 1989). They got their names
from popular words for sports enthusiasts and drug users, though in other
places they may have other names: Jocks are also known as *soshes, preppies,*
or *sloanes;* Burnouts are also called *hoods, greasers, freaks,* or *spacers.* The

speech link between East Belfast men and West Belfast women is discussed in J. Milroy and L. Milroy, 'Linguistic change, social network and speaker innovation', in *Journal of Linguistics* 21 (1985), pp. 339–84. Belfast English is discussed in greater depth in L. Milroy, *Language and social networks*, 2nd edition (Oxford: Blackwell, 1987) and J. Milroy, *Linguistic variation and change: On the historical sociolinguistics of English* (Oxford: Blackwell, 1992).

ESTUARY ENGLISH: The term *Estuary English* was coined by David Rosewarne, and became widely known following an article 'Estuary English' written by him which was published in the *Times Educational Supplement*, 19 October 1984. In it, he described Estuary English as 'a variety of modified regional speech. It is a mixture of non-regional and local south-eastern English pronunciation and intonation.' The 'estuary' is the Thames Estuary, though the speakers of this variety of English now extend well beyond the strict Thames Estuary area. A popular account of the characteristics of this speech is found in P. Coggle, *Do you speak Estuary? The new Standard English* (London: Bloomsbury, 1993).

LOSS OF WORD ENDINGS IN LATIN: Latin words in -*um* such as *vinum* lost their final -*m*, and -*u* changed to -*o*, as in Latin *vino*. In French *vin* the final vowel -*o* has been lost, and so now has the *n*, which is retained only as a trace in the now nasalized vowel in *vin*.

BONK, YOMP, WIMP: *Bonk*: its spread and possible etymology are discussed in J. Ayto, *The Longman register of new words*, vol. 1 (London: Longman, 1989). *Yomp, wimp*: These terms are term listed in J. Ayto and J. Simpson, *The Oxford dictionary of modern slang* (Oxford: Oxford University Press, 1992).

LIFE-COMPANION WORDS: According to John Simpson, editor of the *Oxford English Dictionary* (personal communication), *posslq* was possibly coined in 1978 by Arthur Norton of US Bureau of Censuses for *Time* Magazine for talking about partners on census forms. It is still used intermittently, for example, in the *Independent on Sunday*, 10 October 1993, where it was spelled *possleque*.

TO LASH THE WIND: Samuel Johnson's claim that 'enchaining syllables' was like 'lashing the wind' is found in the preface to his dictionary.

2 A web of deceit

ORIGIN OF LANGUAGE: The origin of language is explored more fully in J. Aitchison, *The seeds of speech: Language origin and evolution* (Cambridge:

Cambridge University Press, 1996), which elaborates on many of the points made in this chapter, and provides numerous suggestions for further reading, some of which are outlined below.

QUOTATION: The quotation by Edward Tylor at the head of the chapter is from a paper published in the *Fortnightly Review* 1866, reprinted in R. Harris (editor), *The origin of language* (Bristol: Thoemmes, 1996), pp. 81–99. The quotation appears on p. 82.

OLD IDEAS: The story of Psammetichus is related by the Greek historian Herodotus in his *Histories*, book 2, chapter 1–2. The views of John Webb and Abbot O'Donnelly are reported in M. Yaguello, *Lunatic lovers of language: Imaginary languages and their inventors* (London: Athlone, 1984/91. First published as *Les fous du langage: des langues imaginaires et de leurs inventeurs*, Paris: Editions du Seuil, 1984). They are among those whom she labels 'lunatic lovers of language'. William Dwight Whitney stated that views on the origin of language were 'mere windy talk' in W. D. Whitney, *Oriental and linguistic studies*, vol. 1. (New York: Charles Scribner's Sons, 1893), p. 279. Locke's claim that language is a 'great conduit' comes in J. Locke, *An essay concerning human understanding* (Oxford: Clarendon Press, 1690/1975).

LANGUAGE WEAKNESSES: Hilaire Belloc's comment on knots is quoted in W. H. Auden and L. Kronenberger, *The Faber book of aphorisms* (London: Faber Paperbacks, 1962/70). The language of pain quotation is from Martin Amis, *London Fields* (London: Penguin, 1989/90), p. 349. The language of emotion quotation is from S. Orbach, 'When disappointment strikes', *Guardian Weekend*, 27 May 1994, p. 12.

SOLIDARITY-SPEAK: The notion of 'grooming talk' is found in D. Morris, *The naked ape* (London: Jonathan Cape, 1967). The interchange with Motty occurs in P. G. Wodehouse, *Carry on, Jeeves* (London: Vintage, 1925/91). Panthoots are presumed to be solidarity calls in a report by M. F. Small, 'Ay up, a chimp wi' an accent', in *New Scientist* (4 June 1994), pp. 33–7. The remark about the 'peculiar human habit of continually stating and restating the very obvious' is from Douglas Adams, *The restaurant at the end of the Universe* (London: Pan, 1980), p. 123.

TURN-TAKING: On conversational turn-taking in modern English, see S. Levinson, *Pragmatics* (Cambridge: Cambridge University Press, 1983), chapter 6; D. Schiffrin, *Approaches to discourse* (Oxford: Blackwell, 1994), chapter 7; G. Button and J. R. E. Lee, *Talk and social organization* (Clevedon, Avon: Multilingual Matters, 1987).

LYING AND MACHIAVELLIAN INTELLIGENCE: Evidence for 'Machiavellian intelligence' in primates is put forward in R. W. Byrne and A. Whiten, 'Cognitive evolution in primates: Evidence from tactical deception', in *Man* 27 (1992), pp. 609–27, and R. W. Byrne, 'The ape legacy: The evolution of Machiavellian intelligence and interactive planning', in E. Goody (editor), *Social intelligence and interaction* (Cambridge: Cambridge University Press, 1994); 'Matilda, who told Lies and was Burned to Death' by Hilaire Belloc is from *Selected cautionary verses* (London: Pelican, 1940/64). Mrs Skewton, for whom yawning was 'a demonstration of delight', occurs in Charles Dickens, *Dombey and son*, vol. 1, chapter 27.

SUPPRESSION OF SPONTANEOUS CALLS: The suppression of copulatory calls by Papoose and Titus is documented in R. W. Byrne. 'The evolution of intelligence', in P. J. B. Slater and T. R. Halliday (editors), *Behaviour and evolution* (Cambridge: Cambridge University Press, 1994). The anecdote about Figan and the banana occurs in J. Goodall, *The chimpanzees of Gombe: Patterns of behaviour* (Cambridge, MA: Harvard University Press, 1986).

HUMAN SOUND-MAKING ABILITY: This is discussed in L. Aiello and C. Dean, *An introduction to human evolutionary anatomy* (London: Academic Press, 1990); P. Lieberman, *The biology and evolution of language* (Cambridge, MA: Harvard University Press, 1984) and P. Lieberman, *Uniquely human: The evolution of speech, thought and selfless behavior* (Cambridge, MA: Harvard University Press, 1991) – though Lieberman's claims are controversial.

HUMANS AND BIRDS: James Burnett Lord Monboddo claimed that humans learned to sing and speak from birds in his mammoth (6 volume) work *The origin and progress of language* (Edinburgh: A. Kincaid, 1773). Sections of it are quoted and summarized in G. Fano, *The origins and nature of language* (Bloomington: Indiana University Press, 1992, translated by S. Petrilli. First published as *Origini e natural del linguaggio*, 1962 and 1973). F. Nottebohm, 'A zoologist's view of some language phenomena with particular emphasis on vocal learning', in E. H. Lenneberg and E. Lenneberg (editors), *Foundations of language development*, vol. 1 (New York: Academic Press, 1975), points out similarities between birdsong and human language. P. Marler, 'Differences in behavioural development in closely related species: birdsong' in P. Bateson (editor), *The development and integration of behaviour* (Cambridge: Cambridge University Press, 1991), discusses the white-crowned sparrow.

TALKING DRUMS: 'Talking drums' are discussed in J. F. Carrington, 'The talking drums of Africa', in *Scientific American* (December 1971), pp. 90–4, which provided the source for the information in figure 2.1. A 'whistle language' on the Canary Island La Gomera works in a somewhat similar manner: it conveys messages via variation in pitch. Its workings are outlined in A. Classe, 'The whistled language of La Gomera', in *Scientific American* (April 1957), pp. 111–20.

OUT OF AFRICA: Information from DNA and blood groups which supports the 'out of Africa' hypothesis is summarized in R. Lewin, *The origin of modern humans* (New York: Scientific American Library, 1993). The 'East Side' scenario is outlined in Y. Coppens, 'East Side story: The origin of humankind', in *Scientific American* 270 (5 May 1994), pp. 62–79. The Robert Frost quotation is from the poem 'The road not taken', in *The poetry of Robert Frost* (London: Jonathan Cape, 1969/71), p. 105.

FIRST WORDS: Darwin's speculation that an 'unusually wise ape-like animal' imitated the growl of a beast of prey is in C. Darwin, *The descent of man and selection in relation to sex*, vol. 1–2 (London: John Murray, 1871), p. 85. The so-called *pooh-pooh*, *ding-dong* and *yo-he-yo* theories of language origin became widely known from O. Jespersen, *Language, its nature, development and origin* (London: Allen Unwin, 1922), who was summarizing work by the German linguist F. Max Müller, who tried to classify views on language origin into various types, apparently pouring scorn on these various theories.

SOUNDS AS SYMBOLS: Vervet monkey danger calls (fig. 2.3) are discussed in R. M. Seyfarth, D. L. Cheney and P. Marler, 'Monkey responses to three different alarm calls: Evidence for predator classification and semantic communication', in *Science* 210 (1980), pp. 801–3, and R. M. Seyfarth, D. L. Cheney and P. Marler, 'Vervet monkey alarm calls: Semantic communication in a free-ranging primate', in *Animal Behavior* 28 (1980), pp. 1070–94. Squirrel monkey danger calls are outlined in D. W. Ploog, 'The evolution of vocal communication', in H. Papousek, U. Jürgens and M. Papousek (editors), *Nonverbal communication: Comparative and developmental approaches* (Cambridge: Cambridge University Press, 1992).

ORDER PREFERENCES IN CHIMP SIGNING: Nim Chimpsky's random signing order with occasional preferences, such as 'food first', is documented in H. S. Terrace, *Nim* (New York: Knopf, 1979). The possible ordering sequence invented by Kanzi, a bonobo chimp, is described in E. S. Savage-Rumbaugh and R. Lewin, *Kanzi: The ape at the brink of the human mind* (New York: Doubleday, 1994).

HUMAN MIND-SET: The human preference for locating 'small on large' is discussed in B. Landau and R. Jackendoff, '"What" and "where" in spatial language and spatial cognition', in *Behavioral and Brain Sciences* 16(2) (1993), pp. 217–65, and in R. Jackendoff, *Patterns in the mind : Language and human nature* (New York: Basic Books, 1993/4). The human 'animate first' and 'verb-object closeness' tendencies are discussed in R. S. Tomlin, *Basic word order: Functional principles* (London: Croom Helm, 1986) – though claims about human preferences are notoriously controversial, since languages differ so much, at least at a superficial level.

MISKITU INDIANS: The comments on the sophistication of the language of the Miskitu Indians are in C. N. Bell, *Tangweera: Life and adventures among gentle savages* (London: Arnold, 1899).

3 Building the web

CHILD LANGUAGE: J. Aitchison, *The articulate mammal: An introduction to psycholinguistics*, 3rd edition (London: Routledge, 1989) elaborates on a number of points made in this chapter. For a non-technical outline aimed at parents, see D. Crystal, *Listen to your child: A parent's guide to children's language* (London: Penguin, 1986). S. Pinker, *The language instinct: The new science of language and mind* (London: Allen Lane, 1994) also discusses the biological basis of language. The following are useful books of readings on various aspects of child language: J. Berko Gleason (editor), *The development of language*, 3rd edition (New York: Macmillan, 1993); P. Bloom (editor), *Language acquisition: Core readings* (Cambridge, MA: MIT Press, 1994); P. Fletcher and B. MacWhinney (editors), *The handbook of child language* (Oxford: Blackwell, 1995).

QUOTATIONS: The quotation at the top of the chapter is from Martin Amis, *London Fields* (London: Jonathan Cape, 1989; London: Penguin, 1990), pp. 223–4. The quotation about ET is from William Kotzwinkle, *E.T.: The Extra-Terrestrial* (London: Sphere, 1982), p. 102. The comment 'Teach your child to hold his tongue; he'll learn fast enough to speak' is attributed to Benjamin Franklin.

CRYING: 'A loud noise at one end and no sense of responsibility at the other' is attributed to Ronald Knox by the *Bloomsbury thematic dictionary of quotations* (London: Bloomsbury, 1988), p. 33. The world-wide similarity of children's crying is pointed out in B. M. Lester and C. F. Boukydis, 'No language but a cry', in H. Papousek, U. Jürgens and M. Papousek (editors), *Nonverbal vocal communication: Comparative and developmental*

approaches (Cambridge: Cambridge University Press, 1992). Deafened
ringdoves which start another brood are referred to in F. Nottebohm, 'A
zoologist's view of some language phenomena with particular emphasis on
vocal learning', in E. H. Lenneberg and E. Lenneberg (editors), *Foundations
of language development*, vol. 1. (New York: Academic Press, 1975).

BABBLING: *Papa* and *mama* as early babbles to which parents attribute meaning
are pointed out by R. Jakobson, 'Why "mama" and "papa"?', in A. Bar-Adon
and W. F. Leopold (editors), *Child language: A book of readings* (Englewood
Cliffs, NJ: Prentice-Hall, 1962/71). The nineteenth-century scholar
Hippolyte Taine spoke of his daughter 'twittering like a bird' in an article
in the periodical *Mind* (1877), reprinted in A. Bar-Adon and W. F. Leopold
(eds.), *Child language: A book of readings* (Englewood Cliffs, NJ: Prentice-
Hall, 1971), a book which reprints a number of early articles on child language. A huge literature on babbling now exists: M. M. Vihman, M. A.
Macken, R. Miller, H. Simmons and J. Miller, 'From babbling to speech: A
re-assessment of the continuity issue', in *Language* 61 (1985), pp. 397–445,
and M. M. Vihman, *Phonological development: The origins of language
in the child* (Oxford: Blackwell, 1996) give a useful overview.

EARLY WORDS AND THE NAMING INSIGHT: Early words are discussed in M.
Barrett, 'Early lexical development', in P. Fletcher and B. MacWhinney
(editors), *The handbook of child language* (Oxford: Blackwell, 1995). J.
McShane, *Learning to talk* (Cambridge: Cambridge University Press, 1980)
discusses the sometimes late development of the 'naming insight'. Helen
Keller's account of her naming insight comes in H. Keller, *The story of my
life* (New York: Doubleday, 1903). The *sand* examples are from M. D. S.
Braine, *Children's first word combinations* (Monograph of the Society for
Research in Child Development 41.1, Chicago: University of Chicago
Press, 1976).

WORD-ENDINGS AND PRONOUNS: The *wug* test was devised by J. Berko, 'The
child's learning of English morphology', in *Word* 14 (1958), pp. 150–77 (also
in Bar-Adon and Leopold, *Child language*). Sophie's speech development,
including her word endings, is described in P. Fletcher, *A child's learning
of English* (Oxford: Basil Blackwell, 1985). The development of pronouns is
documented by S. Chiat, 'Personal pronouns', in P. Fletcher and M. Garman
(editors), *Language acquisition*, 2nd edition (Cambridge: Cambridge
University Press, 1986).

MATURATIONALLY CONTROLLED BEHAVIOUR: The 'classic' book which discussed this was E. H. Lenneberg (editor), *Biological foundations of language* (New York: Wiley, 1967). Most people nowadays speak of 'innately guided behaviour', which is explained in S. J. Gould and P. Marler, 'Learning by instinct', in *Scientific American* 256(1) (1987), pp. 62–73: Gould and Marler point out that humans instinctively pay attention to certain aspects of speech, just as bees pay attention to particular aspects of flowers (fig. 3.2). The ability of the 'cocktail-party chatterer' Laura is discussed in J. L. Yamada, *Laura: A case for the modularity of language* (Cambridge, MA: MIT Press, 1990).

SENSITIVE PERIOD: The French research showing that children could distinguish French from other languages in the first week of their life is reported in J. Mehler, P. Jusczyk, G. Lambertz, N. Halsted, J. Bertoncini and C. Amiel-Tison, 'A precursor of language acquisition in young infants', in *Cognition* 29 (1988), pp. 143–78. The 'filter hypothesis' is proposed in E. L. Newport, 'Contrasting conceptions of the critical period for language', in S. Carey and R. Gelman (editors), *The epigenesis of mind: Essays on biology and cognition* (Cambridge, MA: MIT Press, 1991). The vocabulary spurt is discussed in the next chapter.

PARAMETER SETTING ('SETTING SWITCHES'): Chomsky's parameter setting is outlined in J. Aitchison, *Linguistics: An introduction* (London: Hodder and Stoughton, 1995), also published under the title: *Linguistics*, 4th edition (London: Hodder and Stoughton (Teach Yourself Books), 1995). Chomsky himself outlines his theory in a readable way in N. Chomsky, *Knowledge of language: Its nature, origin and use* (New York: Praeger, 1986). J. M. Meisel, 'Parameters in acquisition', in Fletcher and MacWhinney (1995), *Handbook of child language*, provides an update, putting forward both the pros and the cons of the theory.

CAREGIVER SPEECH: An overview of issues in CDS 'child directed speech' is provided by C. E. Snow, 'Issues in the study of input: Finetuning, universality, individual and developmental differences, and necessary causes', in Fletcher and MacWhinney, *Handbook of child language*. The early research on caregiver language which reported on what parents tend to correct was R. Brown, C. Cazden and U. Bellugi, 'The child's grammar from I to III', in J. P. Hill (editor), *Minnesota symposium on child psychology*, vol. 2 (Minneapolis: University of Minnesota Press, 1968). This paper also suggested that you might expect children to grow up speaking the truth ungrammatically. The 'baby rabbits' quotation is in C. Cazden, *Child*

language and education (New York: Holt, Rinehart and Winston, 1972).
G. Wells and W. P. Robinson, 'The role of adult speech in language development', in C. Fraser and K. R. Scherer (editors), *Advances in the social psychology of language* (Cambridge: Cambridge University Press, 1982) was another early paper which suggested that talking about 'joint interests' was important, and that parents tended to talk to girls more than boys. Vincent, the hearing child of deaf parents, was reported on in P. Todd and J. Aitchison, 'Learning language the hard way', in *First Language* 1 (1980), pp. 122–40.

STANDARD ENGLISH: Standard English is discussed in T. Crowley, *Standard English and the politics of language* (Urbana: University of Illinois, 1989). Readings relating to the prescriptive-descriptive debate (chapter 1) are also relevant. See also Christopher Brumfit, *Standard English*, briefing document compiled by the Centre for Language in Education, School of Education, University of Southampton, Southampton SO17 1BJ; also D. M. Engel and M. R. Whitehead, 'Which English? Standard English and language variety: Some educational perspectives', in *English in Education* 30.1 (1996), pp. 36–49. In England, there is a Council which sets up a National Curriculum for schools: as explained in the chapter, it has recently made it clear that it recognizes that Standard English is NOT an accent.

FOR YOU AND I: Discussions about whether to use *I* or *me* in the phrases *you and I*, or *you and me* attracted more comments than any other topic according to David Crystal, 'Language on the air – has it degenerated?', in *The Listener*, 9 July 1981. The Lady Thatcher use of *for you and I* as well as similar uses by other well-known figures are documented in John Honey, 'A new rule for the Queen and I?', in *English Today* 44 (October 1995), pp. 3–8.

AGARD: The extract is from John Agard's poem 'The wanted man' (New Poems) in *Mangoes and Bullets: Selected and new poems* (London: Pluto Press, 1985), p. 44.

4   A web of words

WORDS IN THE HUMAN MIND: The human wordstore 'the mental lexicon' is the topic of J. Aitchison, *Words in the mind: An introduction to the mental lexicon*, 2nd edition (Oxford: Blackwell, 1994), which contains further references to work on many of the topics discussed in this chapter.

QUOTATIONS: The quotation at the head of the chapter is from Penelope Lively, *Moontiger* (London: André Deutsch, 1987; London: Penguin, 1988), p. 43

and 51. Dean Farrar's comment is in F. W. Farrar, *Chapters on language* (London: Longmans Green, 1865), p. 59.

NUMBER OF WORDS: A guesstimate of 60,000 as the vocabulary size of an educated American adult is made in G. A. Miller and P. M. Gildea, 'How children learn words', *Scientific American* 257.3 (1987), pp. 86–91. My own informal testing with British university students suggests a minimum of 50,000 words as potentially active vocabulary. The quotation about the 'child's wizardry' is in S. Carey, 'The child as word learner', in M. Halle, J. Bresnan and G. A. Miller (editors), *Linguistic theory and psychological reality* (Cambridge, MA: MIT Press, 1978).

VIEWS ON WORDS: Dad who carried a tiny blue dictionary is from Hanif Kureshi, *The Buddha of suburbia* (London: Faber and Faber, 1990), p. 28; Evelyn Waugh's claim that words have 'basic inalienable meanings' is quoted in J. Green, *A dictionary of contemporary quotations* (London: Pan Books, 1982). The bureaucratic definition of a *cow* is from a letter to *The Times*.

WORD FUZZINESS: The meaning of a word as something over which the word 'hovers like a gull' was said by the writer R. G. Collingwood, *The principles of art* (Oxford: Oxford University Press, 1938).Wittgenstein's discussion of the 'family resemblance' phenomenon is from L. Wittgenstein, *Philosophical investigations*, 2nd edition (Oxford: Blackwell, 1958). Labov's work on containers is reported in W. Labov, 'The boundaries of words and their meanings', in C.-J. N. Bailey and R. W. Shuy (editors), *New ways of analyzing variation in English* (Washington DC: Georgetown University Press, 1973). Rosch's early influential article on prototypes was E. Rosch, 'Cognitive representations of semantic categories', in *Journal of Experimental Psychology* 104 (1975), pp. 192–233. The child's view of the moon was reported in M. Bowerman, 'The structure and origin of semantic categories in the language learning child', in D. Foster and S. Brandes (editors), *Symbol as sense: New approaches to the analysis of meaning* (New York: Academic Press, 1980). The *rah-rah* was reported by Mary Stastny in a letter to *The Guardian*, 15 November 1980. The responses of children and non-native speakers to a ranking task is reported in J. Aitchison, 'Good birds, better birds and amazing birds: The development of prototypes', in H. Béjoint and P. Arnaud (editors), *Vocabulary and applied linguistics* (London: Macmillan, 1992).

'SLIPS OF THE TONGUE': Freud's example of *closed* for 'opened' is reported in

S. Freud, *The psychopathology of everyday life* translated by A. Tyson (London: Penguin, 1975). Various examples of problems with word meaning are given in M.F. Garrett, 'Disorders of lexical selection', in W. J. M. Levelt (editor), *Lexical access in speech production* (Oxford: Blackwell, 1993, originally published in *Cognition* 42 (1992), pp. 143–80). The inability of some patients to distinguish similar items is discussed in B. Butterworth, D. Howard and P. McLoughlin, 'The semantic deficit in aphasia: The relationship between semantic errors in auditory comprehension and picture naming', in *Neuropsychologia* 22 (1984), pp. 409–26.

OPPOSITES AND SYNONYMS: The fact that opposites often occur together in speech is documented in C. Fellbaum, 'Co-occurrence and antonymy', in *International Journal of Lexicography* 8 (1995), pp. 281–303. The difference between *chase* and *pursue* is explored by J. Aitchison and D. M. Lewis, 'The mental word-web: Forging the links', in J. Svartvik (editor), *Words: Proceedings of an International Symposium, Lund, 25–26 August 1995* (Stockholm: Swedish Academy, 1996). The *chase* and *pursue* examples quoted in the text are from the British National Corpus, a databank of both spoken and written English. The word *wimp* and how it is learned is discussed in J. Aitchison and D. M. Lewis, 'How to handle wimps: Incorporating new lexical items as an adult', in *Folia Linguistica* 29 (1995), pp. 7–20.

CHILDREN VS ADULTS: Differences between adult and child word-storage are discussed in J. Aitchison and M. Straf, 'Lexical storage and retrieval: A developing skill?', in *Linguistics* 19 (1981), pp. 751–95 (also published in A. Cutler (editor), *Slips of the tongue and language production* (Berlin: Mouton, 1982)), and in J. Aitchison and S. Chiat, 'Natural phonology or natural memory? The interaction between phonological processes and recall mechanisms', in *Language and Speech* 24 (1981), pp. 311–26.

NEW WORDS: A *dead-cat bounce* was reported in J. Ayto, *Longman register of new words*, vol. 1 (London: Longman, 1989); *greenism* in J. Ayto, *Longman register of new words*, vol. 2 (London: Longman, 1990); *middlescence* in Gail Sheehy, *Passages*, Dutton 1976; 'I'm an absolute *magaholic*', said Toni Rodgers in the *Sunday Times* colour supplement, 11 April 1993. James Bramston's comment that 'expressions rise and fall' occurs in his book, *The art of Politicks, In Imitation of Horace's Art of Poetry* (London: Lawton Gilliver, 1729), p. 7. A child's coinage of *souping* is from E. V. Clark, 'The young word maker: A case study of innovation in the child's lexicon' in E. Wanner and L. R. Gleitman (editors), *Language acquisition: The state of the art* (Cambridge: Cambridge University Press, 1982). *Woggle, wuggable, wuglet, miniwug* are discussed in J. Aitchison, 'Shuddering halt or sudden spurt? The linguistic development of (pre-) adolescents' in *Proceedings of the Singapore Association for Applied Linguistics* (in press). The *mini-/micro-* prefix explosion is described in J. Aitchison, *Language joyriding* (Oxford: Clarendon Press, 1994). The word *manywhere* occurs in the preface to Masayoshi Nagata, *Local rings* (New York: Interscience Publishers, 1962).

MULTI-DIMENSIONAL WORD LINKS: M. T. Motley, 'Slips of the tongue', in *Scientific American* 253 (September, 1985), pp. 114–19, explains how slips of the tongue reveal multi-dimensional links. Michael Frayn's play, 'Alphabetical order' is in *Plays: One* (London: Methuen, 1986).

WORD SEARCHING: The quotation on frustrated word-searching is from Vladimir Nabokov, *Pale fire*, Canto 2, 203–8 (London: Weidenfeld and Nicolson, 1962), p. 40.

5   A world-wide web

SOURCES: This chapter combines a number of different topics. Some of the points made are dealt with in J. Aitchison, 'Free or ensnared? The hidden nets of language', in E. Barker (editor), *LSE on freedom* (London: LSE Books, 1995) and J. Aitchison, *Language joyriding* (Oxford: Clarendon Press, 1994), also in the early chapters of J. Aitchison, *The seeds of speech: Language origin and evolution* (Cambridge: Cambridge University Press, 1996).

QUOTATIONS: The quotation at the beginning of the chapter is from Mary Shelley, *Frankenstein* (London: Bantam, 1818/1981). The quotation about man being the only animal who blushes is from Mark Twain, *Following the equator: A journey around the world* (New York: Dover, 1897; London: Constable, 1989), heading of chapter 27. Mermecolions are described in Jorge Luis Borges, *The book of imaginary beings* (London: Penguin, 1974).

CLOSED SYSTEMS: The closed system of the grasshopper is described in T. A. Sebeok, 'Animal communication', in *Science* 147 (1965), pp. 1006–14.

GOBBLEDEGOOK: The young man who impresses with 'idle chatter of a transcendental kind' is from W. S. Gilbert, *Patience*, Act I. The problem with the term *cardiac arrest* is from page 376 of R. Shuy, 'The medical interview: problems in communication', in *Primary Care* 3 (1976), pp. 365–86 (quoted in C. West and R. M. Frankel, 'Miscommunication in medicine', in N. Coupland, H. Giles and J. M. Wiemann (editors), *Miscommunication and problematic talk* (London: Sage, 1991), pp. 166–94). The personal pension plan which defined 'foreign emoluments' was quoted in the *Sunday Times*, 30 May 1993. Pascal's claim that he did not have time to make his letter shorter is in B. Pascal, 'Lettres provinciales, xvi' (1657), quoted in *The Oxford dictionary of quotations*, 3rd edition (Oxford: Oxford University Press, 1979). The comment by the Member of the European Parliament was quoted in the *Sunday Telegraph*, 11 February 1996.

POLITICAL CORRECTNESS: – EUPHEMISMS. *Workforce imbalance correction* is in J. Ayto, *Euphemisms: Over 3,000 ways to avoid being rude or giving offence* (London: Bloomsbury, 1993). The *fare restructuring* was a notice in a San Francisco bus: 'Effective Aug 17 1981. We are restructuring our fares. The new fare between Berkeley and SFO is being changed from $9 to $11 per person.' The various terms for 'mentally disturbed' (fig. 5.1) are from *The Journal of Forensic Psychiatry* 3.3 (December 1992), mainly from an article by John Ayto, 'Of disturbed and bizarre', pp. 297–9. On political correctness in general, a variety of views are put forward in S. Dunant (editor), *The war of the words: The political correctness debate* (London: Virago, 1994).

THE 'WIMP EFFECT': George Bush and the wimp effect was discussed in J. Aitchison, *Language joyriding* (1994), also in J. Aitchison and D. M. Lewis, 'How to handle wimps: incorporating new lexical items as an adult', in *Folia Linguistica* 29 (1995), pp. 7–20. The report on the enquiry into the New York police force was in the *New York Times*, March 1994.

SAPIR–WHORF HYPOTHESIS: Sapir's claim (1929) that 'humans do not live in the objective world alone' is on p. 162 in E. Sapir, 'The status of linguistics as a science' (1929) in E. Sapir, *Selected writings in language, culture and personality* (Berkeley, CA: University of California Press, 1949), pp. 160–6. 'The great Eskimo vocabulary hoax' is in G. K. Pullum, *The great Eskimo vocabulary hoax and other irreverent essays on the study of language* (Chicago: University of Chicago Press, 1991). Whorf's claim about 'Standard Average European' time is on p. 140 in B. L. Whorf, 'The relation of habitual thought and behavior to language' (1939) in B. L. Whorf, *Language, thought and reality: Selected writings of Benjamin Lee Whorf* (Cambridge, MA: MIT Press, 1956).

HE/SHE PROBLEM: The 'botanist in the field' study was reported in D. G. MacKay and D. Fulkerson, 'On the comprehension and production of pronouns', in *Journal of Verbal Learning and Verbal Behavior* 18 (1979), pp. 661–73. The 'beginning writer' study was reported in D. G. MacKay,

'Psychology, prescriptive grammar and the pronoun problem', in *American Psychologist* 35 (1980), pp. 444–9.

MENTAL MODELS: The notion of *mother* as a cluster of different ideas is in G. Lakoff, *Women, fire and dangerous things: What categories reveal about the mind* (Chicago: Chicago University Press, 1987). The falsity of the 'layer-cake' model of society is explained by R. Dahrendorf, *On Britain* (London: British Broadcasting Corporation, 1982). The quotation about the piano as a symbol of being middle-class was by Rufus Sewell, quoted in 'Sayings of the week', *The Observer*, 19 September 1993. The work on anger is in G. Lakoff, *Women, fire and dangerous things*. Experiments on how people view idioms such as 'hit the roof' were reported in R. W. Gibbs and J. E. O'Brien, 'Idiom and mental imagery: The metaphorical motivation for idiomatic meaning', in *Cognition* 36 (1990), pp. 35–68. Anger as dry heat in India is discussed in C. Osella and P. Osella, 'Sneham and the articulation of bodies' (Seminar paper presented in the Department of Anthropology, London School of Economics and Political Science, 1993). Fear as an empty container is discussed in J. Aitchison, 'Chains, nets or boxes? The linguistic capture of love, anger and fear' in W. G. Busse (editor), *Anglistentag 1991 Düsseldorf, Proceedings* (Berlin: Mouton de Gruyter, 1992).

METAPHORS: 'Nukespeak' is discussed in S. Hilgartner, R. C. Bell and R. O'Connor, *Nukespeak: The selling of nuclear technology in America* (London: Penguin, 1983). The television anecdote is reported in S. H. Elgin, *Genderspeak: Men, women, and the gentle art of verbal self-defense* (New York: Wiley, 1993), p. 146. The 'bingeing' electronics firm was reported by Roger Cowe, 'Bitter 90s pill for Sugar', *The Guardian*, 29 December 1995, p. 2. Comments on appropriacy in wine-tasting notes were made by Giles Kime, editor of *Decanter*, and reported in *The Observer*, *Life* section, 18 June 1985. The wine descriptions in figure 5.3, are from Oz Clarke, *Sainsbury's encyclopaedia of wine: An A-Z guide to the wines of the world* (London: Websters, 1993). Language as a game occurs in F. de Saussure, *Cours de linguistique générale* (Paris: Payot, 1915), English translation by W. Baskin, *Course in general linguistics* (New York: The Philosophical Library, 1959; London: Fontana, 1974), also in L. Wittgenstein, *Philosophical investigations*, 2nd edition (Oxford: Blackwell, 1958). The brain replacing the computer as a model of the mind is proposed in D. E. Rumelhart, G. E. Hinton and J. L. McClelland, 'A general framework for parallel distributed processing', in D. E. Rumelhart and J. L. McClelland (editors), *Parallel distributed processing: Explorations in the microstructure of cognition* (Cambridge: MIT Press, 1986), p. 75.

LANGUAGE LOSS: M. Krauss, 'The world's languages in crisis', in *Language* 68 (1992), pp. 4–10, discusses the rate at which languages are dying, part of a wider study of language loss by K. Hale, C. Craig, N. England, J. LaVerne, M. Krauss, L. Watahomigie and A. Yamamoto, 'Endangered languages', in *Language* 68 (1992), pp. 1–42.

QUOTATION: The 'worry about words' quotation is from A. P. Herbert, *What a word!* (London: Methuen, 1925, 11th edition 1952).

SOURCES OF COMMENTS: The sources/dates of the newspaper comments quoted are: Robert Hanks, *The Independent*, 8 February 1996; A. N. Wilson, *Evening Standard*, 9 February 1996; Mark Lawson, *The Guardian*, 8 February 1996; Robert Hanks, *ibid.*; Harold Jackson, *The Guardian*, 6 February 1996; Paul Johnson, *Daily Mail*, 8 February 1996; Liz Forgan, *Daily Mail*, 12 February 1996; Philip Howard, *The Times*, 9 February 1996; A. N. Wilson, *ibid.*; Paul Johnson, *ibid.*; Sue Gaisford, *The Independent on Sunday*, 10 March 1996. The quotes from letters are brief extracts from private correspondence addressed to me personally, and I have therefore not included the names of the writers.

References

This is an alphabetical list of academic references referred to in the notes. Literary quotations are not included (though they were fully referenced in the notes, in the place in the text in which they occurred).

Aiello, L. and Dean, C. (1990). *An introduction to human evolutionary anatomy.* London: Academic Press.

Aitchison, J. (1989). *The articulate mammal: An introduction to psycholinguistics.* 3rd edn. London: Routledge.

(1991). *Language change: Progress or decay?* 2nd edn. Cambridge: Cambridge University Press.

(1992a). Chains, nets or boxes? The linguistic capture of love, anger and fear. In Busse, W.G. (ed.), *Anglistentag 1991 Düsseldorf, Proceedings.* Berlin: Mouton de Gruyter.

(1992b). Good birds, better birds and amazing birds: The development of prototypes. In Béjoint, H. and Arnaud, P. (eds.), *Vocabulary and applied linguistics.* London: Macmillan.

(1994a). *Language joyriding.* Oxford: Clarendon Press.

(1994b). *Words in the mind: An introduction to the mental lexicon.* 2nd edn. Oxford: Blackwell.

(1995a). Free or ensnared? The hidden nets of language. In Barker, E. (ed.), *LSE on freedom.* London: LSE Books.

(1995b). *Linguistics: An introduction.* London: Hodder and Stoughton, also published under the title: *Linguistics* 4th edition. London: Hodder and Stoughton (Teach Yourself Books).

(1996). *The seeds of speech: Language origin and evolution.* Cambridge: Cambridge University Press.

(in press). Shuddering halt or sudden spurt? The linguistic development of (pre-)adolescents. *Proceedings of the Singapore Association for Applied Linguistics.*

References

Aitchison, J. and Chiat, S. (1981). Natural phonology or natural memory? The interaction between phonological processes and recall mechanisms. *Language and Speech* 24, 311–26.

Aitchison, J. and Lewis, D. M. (1995). How to handle wimps: Incorporating new lexical items as an adult. *Folia Linguistica* 29 (1–2), 7–20.

(1996). The mental word-web: Forging the links. In Svartvik, J. (ed.), *Words: Proceedings of an International Symposium, Lund, 25–26 August 1995*, KVHHA Konferenser 36. Stockholm: Swedish Academy.

Aitchison, J. and Straf, M. (1981). Lexical storage and retrieval: A developing skill? *Linguistics* 19, 751–95. (Also in A. Cutler (ed.) *Slips of the tongue and language production*. Mouton, Berlin, 1982.)

Auden, W.H. and Kronenberger, L. (1962/70). *The Faber book of aphorisms*. London: Faber Paperbacks.

Ayto, J. (1989). *The Longman register of new words*. Vol. 1. London: Longman.

(1990). *The Longman register of new words*. Vol. 2. London: Longman.

(1992). Of disturbed and bizarre. *Journal of Forensic Psychiatry* 3.3, 297–9.

(1993). *Euphemisms: Over 3,000 ways to avoid being rude or giving offence*. London: Bloomsbury.

Ayto, J. and Simpson, J. (1992). *The Oxford dictionary of modern slang*. Oxford: Oxford University Press.

Bailey, R. W. (1992). *Images of English*. Cambridge: Cambridge University Press.

Bar-Adon, A. and Leopold, W. F. (eds.) (1971). *Child language: A book of readings*. Englewood Cliffs, NJ: Prentice-Hall.

Bell, C.N. (1899). *Tangweera: Life and adventures among gentle savages*. London: Arnold.

Berko, J. (1958). The child's learning of English morphology. *Word* 14, 150–77 (also in Bar-Adon and Leopold (1971)).

Berko-Gleason, J. (ed.) (1993). *The development of language*. 3rd edn. New York: Macmillan.

Bloom, P. (ed.) (1994). *Language acquisition: Core readings*. Cambridge, MA: The MIT Press.

Bowerman, M. (1980). The structure and origin of semantic categories in the language learning child. In Foster, D. and Brandes, S. (eds.), *Symbol as sense: New approaches to the analysis of meaning*. New York: Academic Press.

Braine, M. D. S. (1976). *Children's first word combinations*. Chicago: University of Chicago Press. (Monograph of the Society for Research in Child Development, 41.1.)

Brown, R., Cazden, C. and Bellugi, U. (1968). The child's grammar from I to III.

References

In Hill, J.P. (ed.), *Minnesota symposium on child psychology*, vol. II. Minneapolis: University of Minnesota Press. (Also in Brown (1970), Ferguson and Slobin (1973).)

Brumfit, C. (undated). *Standard English*. Briefing document compiled by the Centre for Language in Education, School of Education, University of Southampton, Southampton SO17 1BJ.

Burnett, J. (Lord Monboddo). (1773). *The origin and progress of language*. Vols. 1–6. Edinburgh: A. Kincaid.

Bush, D. (1972). Polluting our language. *American Scholar* Spring 1972, 238–47.

Butterworth, B., Howard, D. and McLoughlin, P. (1984). The semantic deficit in aphasia: The relationship between semantic errors in auditory comprehension and picture naming. *Neuropsychologia* 22, 409–26.

Button, G. and Lee, J. R. E. (1987). *Talk and social organization*. Clevedon, Avon: Multilingual Matters.

Byrne, R. W. (1994a). The ape legacy: The evolution of Machiavellian intelligence and interactive planning. In Goody, E. (ed.), *Social intelligence and interaction*. Cambridge: Cambridge University Press.

(1994b). The evolution of intelligence. In Slater, P. J. B. and Halliday, T. R. (eds.), *Behaviour and evolution*. Cambridge: Cambridge University Press.

Byrne, R. W. and Whiten, A. (1992). Cognitive evolution in primates: Evidence from tactical deception. *Man* 27, 609–27.

Cameron, D. (1995). *Verbal hygiene*. London: Routledge.

Carey, S. (1978). The child as word learner. In Halle, M., Bresnan, J. and Miller, G. A. (eds.), *Linguistic theory and psychological reality*. Cambridge, MA: MIT Press.

Carrington, J. F. (1971). The talking drums of Africa. *Scientific American* 225 (6, December), 90–4.

Cazden, C. (1972). *Child language and education*. New York: Holt, Rinehart and Winston.

Censor (c.1880/1982). *Don't: A manual of mistakes and improprieties more or less prevalent in conduct and speech*. Whitstable: Pryor Publications.

Chomsky, N. (1986). *Knowledge of language: Its nature, origin and use*. New York: Praeger.

Clark, E.V. (1982). The young word maker: A case study of innovation in the child's lexicon. In Wanner, E. and Gleitman, L. R. (eds.), *Language acquisition: The state of the art*. Cambridge: Cambridge University Press.

Classe, A. (1957). The whistled language of La Gomera. *Scientific American* 196 (4, April), 111–20.

References

Coggle, P. (1993). *Do you speak Estuary?* London: Bloomsbury.

Collingwood, R. G. (1938). *The principles of art.* Oxford: Oxford University Press.

Coppens, Y. (1994). East Side story: The origin of humankind. *Scientific American* 270 (5, May), 62–79.

Cottle, B. (1969). *The triumph of English.* London: Blandford Press.

Crowley, T. (1989). *The politics of discourse: The standard language question in British cultural debates.* London: Macmillan. (Published in the U.S.A. under the title *Standard English and the politics of language,* Urbana: University of Illinois.)

Crystal, D. (1981). Language on the air – has it degenerated? *The Listener,* 9 July 1981.

 (1986). *Listen to your child: A parent's guide to children's language.* London: Penguin.

Dahrendorf, R. (1982). *On Britain.* London: British Broadcasting Corporation.

Darwin, C. (1871). *The descent of man and selection in relation to sex.* Vols. 1–2. London: John Murray.

Dunant, S. (ed.) (1994). *The war of the words: The political correctness debate.* London: Virago.

Eckert, P. (1988). Adolescent social structure and the spread of linguistic change. *Language in Society* 17, 183–207.

 (1989). *Jocks and Burnouts: Social categories and identity in the high school.* New York: Teachers College Press.

Elgin, S. H. (1993). *Genderspeak: Men, women and the gentle art of verbal self-defense.* New York: Wiley.

Engel, D. M. and Whitehead, M. R. (1996). Which English? Standard English and language variety: Some educational perspectives. *English in Education* 30 (1), 36–49.

Fano, G. (1992). *The origins and nature of language.* Bloomington: Indiana University Press. (Trans. Susan Petrilli. Originally *Origini e natural del linguaggio* (1962 and 1973).)

Farrar, F. W. (1865). *Chapters on language.* London: Longmans Green.

Fellbaum, C. (1995). Co-occurrence and antonymy. *International Journal of Lexicography* 8, 281–303.

Fletcher, P. (1985). *A child's learning of English.* Oxford: Basil Blackwell.

Fletcher, P. and Garman, M. (eds.) (1986). *Language acquisition: Studies in first language development.* 2nd edn. Cambridge: Cambridge University Press.

References

Fletcher, P. and MacWhinney, B. (eds.) (1995). *The handbook of child language*. Oxford: Blackwell.

Fowler, H. W. (1926). *Modern English usage*. Oxford: Oxford University Press.

Freud, S. (1975). *The psychopathology of everyday life*. Harmondsworth: Penguin. (Trans. A. Tyson.)

Garrett, M. F. (1993). Disorders of lexical selection. In Levelt, W. J. M. (ed.), *Lexical access in speech production*. Oxford: Blackwell. (Originally published in *Cognition* 42 (1992), 143–80.)

Gibbs, R. W. and O'Brien, J. E. (1990). Idiom and mental imagery: The metaphorical motivation for idiomatic meaning. *Cognition* 36, 35–68.

Gimson, A. C. and Cruttenden, A. (1994). *Gimson's pronunciation of English*. 5th edn. London: Arnold. (Revised by A. Cruttenden.)

Goodall, J. (1986). *The chimpanzees of Gombe: Patterns of behavior*. Cambridge, MA: Harvard University Press.

Gould, S. J. (1983/4). *Hens' teeth and horses' toes*. Harmondsworth: Penguin.

Gould, S. J. and Marler, P. (1987). Learning by instinct. *Scientific American* 256 (1), 62–73.

Graddol, D. and Swann, J. (1982). Trapping linguists. *Language and Communication* 2, 95–111.

Green, J. (1982). *A dictionary of contemporary quotations*. London: Pan Books.

Hale, K., Craig, C., England, N., LaVerne, J., Krauss, M., Watahomigie, L. and Yamamoto, A. (1992). Endangered languages. *Language* 68, 1–42.

Harris, R. (1996). *The origin of language*. Bristol: Thoemmes.

Herbert, A.P. (1925/1952). *What a word!* 11th edn. London: Methuen.

Hilgartner, S., Bell, R. C. and O'Connor, R. (1983). *Nukespeak: The selling of nuclear technology in America*. Harmondsworth: Penguin.

Honey, J. (1995). A new rule for the Queen and I? *English Today* 44, 3–8.

Jackendoff, R. (1993/4). *Patterns in the mind: Language and human nature*. New York: Basic Books.

Jakobson, R. (1971). Why 'mama' and 'papa'? In Bar-Adon, A. and Leopold, W.F. (eds.), *Child language: A book of readings*. Englewood Cliffs, NJ: Prentice-Hall. (First published 1962.)

Jespersen, O. (1922). *Language, its nature, development and origin*. London: Allen Unwin.

Johnson, S. (1755). *A dictionary of the English language*. London: Knapton, Longman et al. (Facsimile published 1990 by Longman Group UK Ltd. CD-ROM published 1996 by Cambridge University Press.)

References

Keller, H. (1903). *The story of my life*. New York: Doubleday.

Krauss, M. (1992). The world's languages in crisis. *Language* 68, 4–10.

Labov, W. (1973). The boundaries of words and their meanings. In Bailey, C.-J.N. and Shuy, R. W. (eds.), *New ways of analyzing variation in English*. Washington, D C: Georgetown University Press.

Lakoff, G. (1987). *Women, fire and dangerous things: What categories reveal about the mind*. Chicago: Chicago University Press.

Landau, B. and Jackendoff, R. (1993). 'What' and 'where' in spatial language and spatial cognition. *Behavioral and Brain Sciences* 16 (2), 217–65. (Includes peer commentary.)

Lenneberg, E. H. (ed.) (1967). *Biological foundations of language*. New York: Wiley.

Lenneberg, E. H. and Lenneberg, E. (eds.) (1975). *Foundations of language development*. Vol. 1–2. New York: Academic Press.

Lester, B. M. and Boukydis, C. F. (1991). No language but a cry. In Papousek, H., Jürgens, U. and Papousek, M. (eds.), *Nonverbal vocal communication: Comparative and developmental approaches*. Cambridge: Cambridge University Press.

Lester, L. and Skousen, R. (1974). The phonology of drunkenness. In *Papers from the Parasession on Natural Phonology*. Chicago: Chicago Linguistics Society.

Levinson, S. (1983). *Pragmatics*. Cambridge: Cambridge University Press.

Lewin, R. (1993). *The origin of modern humans*. New York: Scientific American Library.

Lieberman, P. (1984). *The biology and evolution of language*. Cambridge, MA: Harvard University Press.

(1991). *Uniquely human: The evolution of speech, thought and selfless behavior*. Cambridge, MA: Harvard University Press.

Locke, J. (1690/1975). *An essay concerning human understanding*. Oxford: Clarendon Press.

Lowth, R. (1762/1967). *A short introduction to English grammar*. Menston, England: The Scholar Press. (Facsimile reprint.)

MacKay, D. G. (1980). Psychology, prescriptive grammar and the pronoun problem. *American Psychologist* 35, 444–9.

MacKay, D. G. and Fulkerson, D. (1979). On the comprehension and production of pronouns. *Journal of Verbal Learning and Verbal Behavior* 18, 661–73.

Marler, P. (1991). Differences in behavioural development in closely related

References

species: birdsong. In Bateson, P. (ed.), *The development and integration of behaviour*. Cambridge: Cambridge University Press.

McMahon, A. (1994). *Understanding language change*. Cambridge: Cambridge University Press.

McShane, J. (1980). *Learning to talk*. Cambridge: Cambridge University Press.

Mehler, J., Jusczyk, P., Lambertz, G., Halsted, N., Bertoncini, J. and Amiel-Tison, C. (1988). A precursor of language acquisition in young infants. *Cognition* 29, 143–78.

Meisel, J. M. (1995). Parameters in acquisition. In Fletcher, P. and MacWhinney, B. (eds.), *The handbook of child language*. Oxford: Blackwell.

Miller, G. A. and Gildea, P. M. (1987). How children learn words. *Scientific American* 257 (3), 86–91. (Also in W. S.-Y. Wang (ed.) *The emergence of language: Development and evolution*. W. H. Freeman, New York, 1991.)

Milroy, J. (1992). *Linguistic variation and change: On the historical sociolinguistics of English*. Oxford: Blackwell.

Milroy, J. and Milroy, L. (1985). Linguistic change, social network and speaker innovation. *Journal of Linguistics* 21, 339–84.

(1991). *Authority in language: Investigating language prescription and standardization*. 2nd edn. London: Routledge.

Milroy, L. (1987). *Language and social networks*. 2nd edn. Oxford: Basil Blackwell.

Morris, D. (1967). *The naked ape*. London: Jonathan Cape.

Motley, M. T. (1985). Slips of the tongue. *Scientific American* 253 (September), 114–19.

Müller, F. M. (1861/1994). *Lectures on the science of language*. London: Routledge. (First published 1861 by Thoemmes Press, London.)

Mugglestone, L. (1995). *'Talking proper': The rise of accent as social symbol*. Oxford: Oxford University Press.

Newport, E. L. (1991). Contrasting conceptions of the critical period for language. In Carey, S. and Gelman, R. (eds.), *The epigenesis of mind: Essays on biology and cognition*. Cambridge, MA: MIT Press.

Nottebohm, F. (1975). A zoologist's view of some language phenomena with particular emphasis on vocal learning. In Lenneberg, E. H. and Lenneberg, E. (eds.), *Foundations of language development*, vol. 1. New York: Academic Press.

Osella, C. and Osella, P. (1993). Sneham and the articulation of bodies. Seminar paper presented in the Department of Anthropology, London School of Economics and Political Science.

References

Pascal, B. (1657). Lettres provinciales, xvi. Quoted in *The Oxford dictionary of quotations*, 3rd edn. Oxford: Oxford University Press, 1979.

Payne, R. (1979). Humpbacks: their mysterious songs. *National Geographic* 155 (1 January 1979), 18–25.

Pinker, S. (1994). *The language instinct: The new science of language and mind.* London: Allen Lane.

Ploog, D. W. (1992). The evolution of vocal communication. In Papousek, H., Jürgens, U. and Papousek, M. (eds.), *Nonverbal communication: Comparative and developmental approaches.* Cambridge: Cambridge University Press.

Pullum, G. K. (1991). *The great Eskimo vocabulary hoax and other irreverent essays on the study of language.* Chicago: University of Chicago Press.

Rosch, E. (1975). Cognitive representations of semantic categories. *Journal of Experimental Psychology* 104, 192–233.

Rumelhart, D. E., Hinton, G. E. and McClelland, J. L. (1986). A general framework for parallel distributed processing. In Rumelhart, D. E. and McClelland, J.L. (eds.), *Parallel distributed processing: Explorations in the microstructure of cognition.* Cambridge, MA: MIT Press.

Sapir, E. (1929/49). *Selected writings in language, culture and personality.* Berkeley, CA: University of California Press.

Saussure, F. de (1915). *Cours de linguistique générale.* Paris: Payot. (English translation by W. Baskin, *Course in general linguistics.* New York: The Philosophical Library, 1959. London: Fontana 1974.)

Savage-Rumbaugh, E. S. and Lewin, R. (1994). *Kanzi: The ape at the brink of the human mind.* New York: Doubleday.

Schiffrin, D. (1994). *Approaches to discourse.* Oxford: Blackwell.

Sebeok, T. A. (1965). Animal communication. *Science* 147, 1006–14.

Seyfarth, R. M., Cheney, D. L. and Marler, P. (1980a). Monkey responses to three different alarm calls: evidence for predator classification and semantic communication. *Science* 210, 801–3.

(1980b). Vervet monkey alarm calls: Semantic communication in a free-ranging primate. *Animal Behavior* 28, 1070–94.

Shuy, R. (1976). The medical interview: Problems in communication. *Primary Care* 3, 365–86. (Quoted in C. West and R. M. Frankel, 'Miscommunication in medicine', in N. Coupland, H. Giles and J. M. Wiemann (eds.), *Miscommunication and problematic talk*, London: Sage, 1991, pp. 166–94.)

Simon, J. (1981). *Paradigms lost.* London: Chatto and Windus.

References

Small, M. F. (1994). Ay up, a chimp wi' an accent. *New Scientist* (4 June), 33–37.

Snow, C. E. (1995). Issues in the study of input: Finetuning, universality, individual and developmental differences, and necessary causes. In Fletcher, P. and MacWhinney, B. (eds.), *The handbook of child language*. Oxford: Blackwell.

Terrace, H.S. (1979). *Nim*. New York: Knopf.

Todd, P. and Aitchison, J. (1980). Learning language the hard way. *First Language* 1, 122–40.

Tomlin, R. S. (1986). *Basic word order: Functional principles*. London: Croom Helm.

Vihman, M. M. (1996). *Phonological development: The origins of language in the child*. Oxford: Blackwell.

Vihman, M. M., Macken, M. A., Miller, R., Simmons, H. and Miller, J. (1985). From babbling to speech: A re-assessment of the continuity issue. *Language* 61, 397–445.

Wagner, G. (1968). *On the wisdom of words*. London: George Allen and Unwin.

Wells, G. and Robinson, W. P. (1982). The role of adult speech in language development. In Fraser, C. and Scherer, K. R. (eds.), *Advances in the social psychology of language*. Cambridge: Cambridge University Press.

Whitney, W. D. (1893). *Oriental and linguistic studies*. Vol. 1. New York: Charles Scribner's Sons.

Whorf, B. L. (1939/1956). *Language, thought and reality: Selected writings of Benjamin Lee Whorf*. Cambridge, MA: MIT Press.

Wittgenstein, L. (1958). *Philosophical investigations*. 2nd edn. Oxford: Blackwell.

Yaguello, M. (1984/91). *Lunatic lovers of language: Imaginary languages and their inventors*. London: Athlone. (Originally: Les fous du langage: des langues imaginaires et de leurs inventeurs. Paris: Editions du Seuil 1984.)

Yamada, J. L. (1990). *Laura: A case for the modularity of language*. Cambridge, MA: MIT Press.

Index

Index

'ding-dong' theory (of language origin), 35, 114n
displacement, 27
DNA, 32, 114n
double negative, 5, 109n
double-layered (language), 29
down v. *up*, 91
drunken speech, 10, 110n

Earle, John, 6, 109n
early words
   human language origins, 35ff
   child language, 44, 116n
East Side story, 32, 114n
Elgin, Susan, 90f, 123n
English plurals, 14
Eskimos, *see* Inuit
Estuary English, 16, 111n
ET the Extra-Terrestrial, 41, 115n
etiquette, 7, 109n
euphemisms, 82f, 122n
   see also Nukespeak

'family resemblance' phenomenon, 65
Farrar, Dean, 61, 119n
fear, 90, 123n
Figan (chimpanzee), 28, 113n
'filter' or 'natural sieve' hypothesis (child language), 49, 50, 117n
Forgan, Liz, 99, 124n
Fowler, Henry, 7, 109n
Franklin, Benjamin, 41, 115n
Frayn, Michael, 77, 121n
French, 16, 49, 68, 111n
Freud, Sigmund, 68, 119n
'frog-in-a-well' problem, 86
Frost, Robert, 33, 114n

Gaisford, Sue, 104, 124n
game metaphor (for language), 92, 94, 123n
generic *he*, 86, 122n
Gleason, Jean Berko, 45
glottal stop, 10, 16, 102
gobbledegook, 81ff, 121n
graffiti, 14, 110n
grasshopper, 80, 121n
'grooming talking', 24, 112n
Gulf War, 90

haka, 25
Hanks, Robert, 97, 99, 124n
he v. *she*, 86, 122n
Herbert, A. P., 95, 124n
Holmes, Sherlock, ix
Hopi, 85
Howard, Philip, 100, 124n
human mind-set, 115n
humpback whales, 2, 108n

Inca week, 87f
'infectious disease' view, 14, 110n
infinitives, x, 81, 100
information (as role of language), 22f
innately guided learning, 47, 117n
Inuit (Eskimos), x, 85, 122n
Italian, 16, 68

Jackson, Harold, 99, 124n
Jocks and Burnouts, 15, 110n
Johnson, Paul, 99, 102, 124n
Johnson, Samuel, 4, 19f, 100, 108n, 111n

Index

Index

Index